bLOWN
to
BITs

BLOWN
to
BITS

HOW THE NEW ECONOMICS OF INFORMATION TRANSFORMS STRATEGY

PHILIP EVANS

THOMAS S. WURSTER

HARVARD BUSINESS SCHOOL PRESS
BOSTON MASSACHUSETTS

Printed in the United States of America

03 02 01 00 99   5 4 3 2 1

Library of Congress Cataloging-in-Publication Data

Evans, Philip, 1950–
    Blown to bits : how the new economics of information transforms
strategy / Philip Evans and Thomas S. Wurster.
        p.   cm.
    Includes bibliographical references and index.
    ISBN 0-87584-877-X (alk. paper)
    1. Information technology.   2. Knowledge management.   3. Strategic
planning.   I. Wurster, Thomas S.   II. Title.
HC79.I55E93   1999
658.4'012—dc21   99-31132
                                                                    CIP

The paper used in this publication meets the requirements of the American
National Standard for Permanence of Paper for Publications and Documents
in Libraries and Archives Z39.48-1992.

This book is dedicated to Jenny, Hayley, and David
—They endured.

contents

PReface

Our clients prompted us to write this book. They asked us questions we could not readily answer: questions relating to the rise of electronic networks and the "information revolution." *Strategy* questions. Dilemmas in managing the transition to new distribution channels. Responses to new and radically dissimilar competitors. Ways to forestall "commoditization." Worries about losing the customer relationship. Debates over whether and how to establish a new business model that would eat into the foundations of the old. Questions about what—concretely, practically—*to do*.

Is mastering Internet technology the *same kind of thing*, they asked, as mastering mainframe and client-server? Is electronic commerce "merely" another revolution in retailing formats, or is it something fundamentally different? Does the network economy strengthen brands, supplier alliances, customer relationships, and the value of information—or does it obliterate them? More fundamentally, whatever these specific challenges, is the large, well-run corporation really the vehicle for addressing them, or is there, at the heart of what is going on, a challenge to its very existence?

They focused on how manifestly different the thinking, decision making, and managerial processes were on "Internet time." The limitations of standard planning methods. The apparent irrelevance of cash flow. The dominance of tactics over grand strategy. The need for independent-minded managers and highly geared incentives. They expressed deep-seated concerns about the ability of their organizations to cope with changes *in the nature of change itself*.

We tried to fix some still points in this rapidly turning world, but it proved very difficult. "Facts" exhibited a half-life measured in months. Forecasts (our own included) proved little more than intelligent guesses. We tried to escape from the clutter of month-to-month contradiction by thinking long-term and holistically. We put together scenarios. But it proved difficult to connect internally coherent visions of the future with the practical, immediate dilemmas of business strategy.

We tried to make a virtue of necessity by centering our strategic thinking on the very facts of uncertainty and unpredictability. But, again, we had the greatest difficulty in deriving practical implications. "Chaos" may be a powerful paradigm for economists, genuinely high-tech businesses, and venture capitalists who are in the business of making bets. But corporations are instruments for deploying resources strategically, with the advantages inherent in large-scale organization. Without understating the real pervasiveness of uncertainty, it seemed to us *essential* that strategy be based on what is knowable rather than what is unknowable. Embracing chaos is an admission of defeat.

So we were driven into an old-fashioned approach that steered between these various extremes. We focused on a level of abstraction *higher* than that of the currently hot phenomenon, but *lower* than that of the long-term vision. We recognized that every business situation is unique, and therefore there really are no simple and universal prescriptions; but we looked hard for those common principles that are necessary, if not sufficient, for competitive survival. We focused on what is stable and knowable while trying to accommodate the real limitations imposed by uncertainty. Above all (and this is the old-fashioned bit) we focused on *competitive advantage* and its *sustainability* as the key drivers of success.

This took us in a surprising direction. We quickly found that many, if not most, of the traditional principles of strategy apply in the "new" much as they do in the old. Economies of scale, segmentation, and cost position all still work. But the *objects* of those principles are different. We realized that the "objects" of strategy—such as business units, industries, supply chains, customer relationships, organizational structure, and so forth—are held together by a "glue," and that glue is essentially information. The glue gets dissolved by new technologies. Therefore things fall apart. But the resulting fragments follow the same rules they always followed. To use a pretentious metaphor, it is as if one force— say the weak force that binds subatomic particles together— were abolished, but the laws of physics otherwise stayed exactly the same.

This led us to the idea of a "new economics of information": not a qualitatively new body of *principles*, but a rebalancing of *existing* economic forces when one of them (the informational glue) is subtracted. When we looked for it, we saw this logic working in surprising places. When we applied it, we and our clients found real power in addressing strategy dilemmas. When we tried it on our colleagues in The Boston Consulting Group, it (and we) survived.

We took these ideas public with an article, "Strategy and the New Economics of Information," published in the September–October 1997 issue of the *Harvard Business Review*. The favorable reaction to that article, plus a strong sense that we had only scraped the surface of these "new economics," led us to attempt the more ambitious medium of a book.

The Book

This book is intended for three kinds of readers. Our primary audience is the executive in an incumbent business, who is aware of what is happening but not an expert, who is concerned that the old business assumptions may no longer apply, and who needs to understand how new economics change old businesses. Our secondary audience is the entrepreneur who is swimming in this maelstrom every day, for whom tactics seem to swamp strategy, to whom we offer a broader, more strategic perspective within which tactical choices can be sorted out. Our third audience is the academic, to whom we offer the hints (only the hints) of a new dimension of strategy theory.

These are very different audiences, and to address them simultaneously requires some compromise in the writing and perhaps some indulgence by the reader. Those who have read our *HBR* article will note recapitulations, most obviously in chapter 1. Readers familiar with the extensive literature on the information revolution may find the explanation of Moore's Law redundant and even a bit irritating (though we did keep it to two paragraphs). These same readers will find some of our examples familiar. This is deliberate: we believe that the logic we propose penetrates deep into the interplay of competitive forces and that familiar examples are the most effective way to demonstrate this. (We also have introduced some less familiar examples.) Readers looking for Ten Rules for Succeeding in the Information Economy will be disappointed: we believe with some passion that the task of rethinking strategy is specific to each business and cannot be short-circuited by simplistic formulas. Moreover, we describe one logic, not all logics. Blanket pronouncements require a comprehensiveness and completeness of under-standing beyond our modest talents.

Acknowledgments

Our greatest debt must go unrecognized: it is to the individual clients with whom and for whom we developed these ideas and worked through their implementation. Rules of confidentiality must take precedence over acknowledging the greatest professional obligation that we owe.

We have also benefited from the opportunity to share this thinking with audiences of senior executives in forums across the world. Seminars with senior executive groups, general management conferences, industry-focused meetings, and opportunities to speak to MBA students and their teachers have all broadened and sharpened our understanding.

Many colleagues within BCG contributed to this effort. Chris Herman, Jeri Silberman Herman, John Soumbasakis, Aaron Tankersley, and Jason Zajac did the basic research on which so much of this book was developed. Their dogged-ness, willingness to pinch-hit, and commitment to the project, often on top of normal client obligations, were extraordinary. John managed two unruly authors through the painful process of meeting deadlines.

Ben Burnett, Deborah Ellinger, Stuart Grief, Joshua Rymer, and Lynn Segal contributed their deep expertise on financial services. Michael Hansen, Peter Lawyer, and Alex

Nesbitt corrected our naive initial beliefs about health care. Ranch Kimball, Arnon Mishkin, and Craig Moffett provided us with helpful insights into the media industries. Neil Monnery, David Pecaut and Michael Silverstein shared with us their deep expertise on retailing. Felix Barber, Stephen Bungay, Chris Keevil, and Anthony Miles sharpened our initial ideas on the impact of information economics on organization. Carlos Bhola, David Ritter, and Stuart Scantlebury corrected our frequent errors on technology issues. Philippe Amouyal, David Edelman, Dieter Heuskel, and Bob Howard helped to put our early thinking in a broader perspective.

Paul Basile, Willie Burnside, David Edelman, Tom Hout, Ron Nicol, and Michael Silverstein read the manuscript in its entirety and gave us invaluable suggestions on content, architecture, and style.

Carl Stern sponsored the project, encouraged us in our darker days, and originated the coinage "richness and reach." George Stalk, head of BCG's Innovation Marketing and Communication Group, made the time spent on this book possible.

Katherine Andrews and Steve Prokesch ably edited the early drafts of the manuscript, frequently under enormous pressure from deadlines. Sandy Rhee typed numerous transcripts and set up more coast-to-coast conference calls than either of us cares to admit. Marjorie Williams of the Harvard Business School Press steered us through the labyrinthine complexities of writing and revision with a patience that we lamentably failed to match.

We also owe an enormous personal debt to our spouses and families—Jenny and Hayley Edbrooke, and David Allen—for their support, forbearance, and patience. They bring meaning and purpose to what we have accomplished.

None of these individual debts absolves the authors from sole responsibility for the errors that remain.

Beyond these individual contributions, we owe a more amorphous but no less profound debt to all the members of The Boston Consulting Group, both past and present. It is a debt associated with teaching us a certain way of thinking. Bruce Henderson, the founder of BCG, was fond of quoting the remark by Archimedes that given a fulcrum and a lever sufficiently long, he could move the world. Bruce believed passionately in the possibility that strategic thinking could move the world. And he was one of the few strategic thinkers who actually did so. We would not presume to any such claim. But Bruce, and the extraordinary professional community he built, did teach us to aspire.

1

a cautionary tale

I<small>N</small> 1768, T<small>HREE</small> S<small>COTTISH</small> P<small>RINTERS</small> began publishing an integrated compendium of knowledge—the earliest and most famous encyclopedia in the English-speaking world. They called it *Encyclopaedia Britannica*. Since then, *Britannica* has evolved through fifteen editions, and to this day it is generally regarded as the world's most comprehensive and authoritative encyclopedia.

In 1920, Sears, Roebuck and Company, an American mail-order retailer, acquired Britannica and moved its headquarters from Edinburgh to Chicago. Ownership passed to William Benton in 1941, who then willed the company in the early 1970s to the Benton Foundation, a charitable organization whose income supports communications programs at the University of Chicago. *Britannica* grew under its American owners into a serious commercial enterprise while sustaining its reputation as the world's most prestigious and comprehensive encyclopedia. The content was revised every four or five years. Brand extensions, such as atlases and yearbooks, were added. The company built one of the most aggressive and successful direct sales forces in the world. By targeting middle-income families and focusing on their aspirations for their children, the company developed a marketing proposition as compelling as the intellectual content of the product itself.

By 1990, sales of *Britannica's* multivolume sets had reached an all-time peak of about $650 million.[1] Dominant market share, steady if unspectacular growth, generous margins, and a two-hundred-year history all testified to an extraordinarily compelling and stable brand. Since 1990, however, sales of *Britannica,* and of all printed encyclopedias in the United States, have collapsed by over 80 percent.[2] *Britannica* was blown away by a product of the late-twentieth-century information revolution: the CD-ROM.

The CD-ROM came from nowhere and destroyed the printed encyclopedia business. Whereas *Britannica* sells for $1,500 to $2,200 per set (depending on the quality of the binding), CD-ROM encyclopedias, such as Encarta, Grolier, and Compton, list for $50 to $70. But hardly anybody pays even that: the vast majority of copies are given away to promote the sale of computers and peripherals. With a marginal manufacturing cost of $1.50 per copy, the CD-ROM as freebie makes good economic sense. The marginal cost of *Britannica,* in contrast, is about $250 for production plus about $500 to $600 for the salesperson's commission.

Judging from their inaction, Britannica's executives at first seemed to have viewed the CD-ROM encyclopedia as an irrelevance: a child's toy, one step above video games. This perception was entirely reasonable. Microsoft had licensed the text for its encyclopedia from Funk & Wagnalls, whose third-rate, nearly defunct product, surviving as a periodic promotional item in the aisles of supermarkets, was perceived to be a brand so pathetic that Microsoft dropped its name in favor of the ad agency coinage *Encarta*. The addition of public-domain illustrations and scratchy sound recordings too old to bear a copyright (and therefore available at no cost) hardly made for a serious rival to the *Britannica*—or so it seemed.

As revenues plunged, it became obvious that whether they *ought* to be or not, CD-ROM encyclopedias were serious competition. Britannica executives reluctantly considered creating their own CD-ROM product, only to encounter a technology constraint: the content of *Britannica* was too big for the medium. *Encarta*, with its seven million words, could fit easily onto a CD-ROM, with plenty of room for illustrations and interactivity. *Britannica*, however, had more than forty million words. It was impossible to create an interactive version within the capacity limits of a CD-ROM. The technology was not ready for the content, so the company's executives decided to wait.

Months passed. Sales continued to plummet. In response, the company put together a text-only CD-ROM version of *Britannica*, only to encounter another crisis: a revolt by the sales force. Even if priced at a significant premium over *Encarta*, a CD-ROM version of *Britannica* could not possibly generate the $500 to $600 sales commission of the printed product, from which it would so obviously take sales. Indeed, a CD-ROM product would have to be sold through a completely different channel. To avert a revolt by the sales force, Britannica executives decided to bundle the CD-ROM as a free bonus for buyers of the multivolume set. Anyone who wanted to buy the CD-ROM alone would have to pay $1,000.

This decision appeased the sales force briefly, but did nothing to stem the continuing collapse of sales. Losses mounted. There was no apparent strategy. In May of 1995, the Benton Foundation finally put the company up for sale.[3]

For nearly eighteen months, investment bankers tried to find a buyer. Microsoft said no. Technology, media, and information companies all declined. Finally, in 1996, financier Jacob Safra agreed to buy the company, paying less than half of book value.

Morals

The decline and fall of *Encyclopaedia Britannica* is more than a parable about the dangers of complacency. It illustrates what we will call the *new economics of information*: how the evolving technological capabilities for sharing and using information can transform business definitions, industry definitions, and competitive advantage. It illustrates how the most stable of industries, the most focused of business models, and the strongest of brands can be blown to bits by new information technology.

The *Britannica* story contains morals for *all* businesses. The first is obvious: the most venerable can prove the most vulnerable. New information technologies can come from nowhere and demolish brands and businesses that have been established for decades, even centuries. One of the greatest brand names in the English-speaking world was nearly destroyed—in just five years—by a cheap, shiny disc.

The second point is a bit less obvious: the history, the myths, the shared values, and the unreflective presuppositions that define a strong corporate culture can blind business leaders to events that do not fit into their collective mental framework.

Britannica's executives initially scoffed at *Encarta* because its content was based on a promotional item sold in supermarkets. But their own market research told them that the typical encyclopedia is opened less than once a year, once the initial pride in ownership fades. Their own sales-people knew full well that the way to sell an encyclopedia is to play on anxieties: parents trying to "do something" for their kids. The fact that the kid never uses the product is beside the point; parental guilt has been duly assuaged.

But today, when parents are anxious about their children's performance in school, when they feel guilty about not doing enough to help, they buy a computer. The new PC may never be used for anything other than chat rooms and video games, but parental guilt has again been duly salved. It just so happens that the computer costs about the same amount as *Britannica*. And along with that computer comes a CD-ROM drive. And along with the CD-ROM drive come several free CD-ROMs, one of which is a promotional copy of *Encarta*.

In other words, if the fundamental value proposition is assuaging parental guilt, then the fundamental competitor is not *Encarta*, it is the PC. *Encarta* is merely the icing on the cake. Supermarket brands and intellectual content have precious little to do with it. But within the mindset of executives in the business, steeped in a culture of scholarly values and self-confident from a history of unbroken success, it is extraordinarily hard to understand early enough that conventional industry definitions are obsolete.

There is a third lesson: even if the executives of established businesses fully grasp the impact of new technologies, and even if they can reason their way beyond their corporate myths and assumptions, they still face a massive competitive disadvantage arising precisely because they are incumbents. Incumbents are saddled with legacy assets—not just clunky mainframe systems, but sales and distribution systems, bricks and mortar, brands and core competencies. Competing in the face of the new economics of information requires cannibalizing those assets, perhaps even destroying them.

Incumbents hesitate to do that, especially as long as the business has positive margins. Rather, they do complex financial calculations and get bogged down in internal political debates. Insurgents have no such inhibitions.

Britannica's sales force had been built over decades. It was a foundation of competitive advantage and the envy of the industry. It was obsolete. An aggressive strategy for the new medium would have required blowing it up. The company hesitated. Microsoft had no reason to hesitate.

This is a real shift. In the vast majority of traditional competitive situations, *the defense has the advantage*. But when the economics of information are shifting, insurgents are advantaged precisely by their lack of legacy systems, legacy assets, and a legacy mindset. Having nothing to lose becomes an advantage.

The destabilization of competitive advantage is as much an opportunity as it is a threat. It just depends on how strategists choose to look at it. One consequence of the obsolescence of industry and business boundaries is that every incumbent under traditional business definitions is free to play the insurgent under some other definition.

There is a fourth lesson: this is not a *zero-sum* game. The total value of the players can rise—or fall—dramatically. The game can be a massively positive sum: in book retailing, total shareholder value has gone up significantly. It can be a massively negative sum: in the encyclopedia business, shareholder value collapsed, perhaps by an order of magnitude. Britannica clearly lost. But it is not obvious that Microsoft or anybody else won. In dollar terms, sales of encyclopedias of all kinds are one-tenth of what they were in 1990.[4] Microsoft never succeeded in getting to the price point it expected. Consumers rarely trade up from last year's promotional version to this year's fully priced version. Consumers benefit (if they ever use the product), but the industry is essentially destroyed. It is not clear that anybody will ever again write works of scholarship comparable to the greatest editions of *Britannica*—at least not in the same form.

But there is hope. Britannica, under its new management, has produced a moderately successful CD-ROM product. It goes far beyond its competitors, not only in quality and sheer volume, but in transcending the CD-ROM's limitations and connecting directly to the World Wide Web. The new *Britannica* aims to become a—indeed *the*—portal to a universe of high-quality, objective, scholarly material. The brand guarantees, as do few others, the seriousness and reliability of the content. The hope is to rise above the clutter and mediocrity that have proliferated in the early years of the Internet and build anew something of permanent value. The identity of that something and the challenge of building it under the vagaries of shifting economics of information are the themes of this book.

2

information and things

Britannica is an information business, but that does not make it special. *Every* business is an information business. In many businesses not widely considered information businesses, information plays a surprisingly critical role. For example, about one-third of the cost of health care in the United States—some $350 billion—consists of the cost of capturing, storing, processing, and retrieving information: patient records, cost accounting, and insurance claims.[1] By that measure, health care is a larger information industry than the "information" industry.

The physical world of manufacturing is shaped by information. A high-end Mercedes automobile contains as much computing power as a midrange personal computer.[2] Information dominates processes as well as products. It is hard to imagine how even low-tech manufacturers could compete without such information-intensive functions as market research, logistics, and advertising. Inventory and work-in-process are purely physical things, but if information were accurate and timely, factories could operate with a fraction of their current inventory. Inventory is merely the physical correlate of deficient information.

More fundamentally, information and the mechanisms for delivering it are the glue that holds together the structure of businesses. Andrew Carnegie and Henry Ford struggled with the cost and difficulty of coordinating large-scale, complex operations. They solved the problem through proprietary information systems and hierarchic control. This gave rise to the vertically integrated value chain, defined as the sequence of activities that a business performs to design, produce, market, deliver, and support its product.

From the time of Alfred P. Sloan, companies developed control systems that enabled efficient decentralization of operations but centralized management of what were later called "synergies" or "core competencies." This shaped the horizontally integrated multidivisional corporation, held together by a logic that transcended the business unit. That logic is essentially informational—the fact that certain kinds of information can be shared more efficiently *within* the boundaries of a corporation than *across* them.[3]

Corporations in turn ally with each other to form the supply chains that define an industry. Supply chains link supplier and customer corporations together. They are shaped by the same kind of informational logic as the value chains within companies, but in a weaker form. When two companies build a long-term relationship, they establish channels for the rich communication of information. These channels may be personal acquaintances among executives or sales and purchasing staff, mutual understandings that are implicit or written into contracts, a dedicated electronic data interchange (EDI) system, collaboration among engineering teams, or mutually synchronized production systems. All, in different ways, are information channels.

A consumer franchise similarly describes the proprietary information that a company has about its customers and that customers have about the company. Brands are the information—whether real or imagined, intellectual or emotional—that consumers associate with a product. And the tools used to build brands—advertising, promotion, sales pitches, even the presentation of goods on a supermarket shelf—are themselves channels for delivering information.

The formal organizational structure of any company is fundamentally a set of channels for the rich exchange of information among employees. Many informal aspects of organizations—the ways in which people work around official lines of communication, develop tacit understandings, and trade moral capital—are also methods of processing information.[4]

"Information," in all these contexts, does not just mean *data*. Qualitative judgments, affiliation, and emotion are all part and parcel of information we exchange, and are inextricably intertwined with the sharing of numbers and facts. Denotation and connotation are fundamentally inseparable.

When we picture value and supply chains, we tend to visualize a linear flow of physical activities. But it is *information*, in the broadest sense of the word, that flows across these activities and binds them together. Information flows ultimately determine what is inside and what is outside the business unit, value chain, supply chain, consumer franchise, and organization.[5]

Competitive Advantage

We live, as everybody knows, in an increasingly information-intensive economy; the contribution of information to GNP is high and clearly rising. But what is even more striking is the extent to which information makes a vastly disproportionate contribution to competitive advantage.

Some of the most admired companies in businesses far removed from the so-called information industries owe most of their success to their masterful use of information. Toyota built powerful competitive advantages through simultaneous engineering, *kanban,* and quality control—all techniques for processing information. American Airlines used its control of the SABRE reservation system to achieve higher levels of capacity utilization.[6] Wal-Mart exploited its EDI links with suppliers and the logistical technique of cross-docking to achieve dramatic increases in inventory turns.[7] Nike employed advertising, celebrity endorsements, and the microsegmentation of its market to transform sneakers into high-priced fashion goods. Coca-Cola, reputedly the most admired corporation in America, excels at one thing—managing the brand.[8] And all the thousands of companies that have embraced Total Quality Management, reengineered their operations, and leveraged their core competencies have chosen to define their managerial goals in terms of flows of information.

In short, information and the mechanisms for delivering it underlie much of what defines business boundaries, stabilizes corporate and industry structures, shapes the organization, and drives competitive advantage. The concepts of value chain and supply chain focus our attention—quite usefully—on the physical sequences that define a business or an industry. But it is information, flowing in the interstices of these chains, that really links them together and generates most of their competitive advantage and profit potential. Like the air we breathe, the importance of information is sometimes overlooked because it is so pervasive, so manifold, and so obvious.

Melting the Glue

Information is the glue that holds value chains and supply chains together. But that glue is now melting. The fundamental cause is the explosion in connectivity and in the information standards that are enabling the open and almost cost-free exchange of a widening universe of rich information. When everyone can communicate richly with everyone else, the narrow, hardwired communications channels that used to tie people together simply become obsolete. And so do all the business structures that created those channels or exploit them for competitive advantage.

The explosion in connectivity has taken almost everyone by surprise. Almost all knowledge workers in the United States have networked personal computers on their office desks. About 50 percent of households in the United States now have personal computers, and more than half of those have connections to the Internet.[9] The daily users of Yahoo! now outnumber viewers of the most popular show on television.[10] By the year 2000, households accounting for about two-thirds of the purchasing power of the domestic economy are expected to have home connections to the Internet.[11]

Broadband connections, such as cable modems and xDSL technologies (which will enable full-motion, switched video), are expected to reach 16 million U.S. households by 2002.[12] By that time, Web-enabled information appliances—personal digital assistants, telephones, set-top boxes, intelligent automobiles, and point-of-sale devices—are expected to outsell personal computers. By 2010, they are expected to outsell PCs by a factor of ten to one.[13]

This phenomenon is not solely American. Currently, over 140 million people worldwide have access to the Internet.[14]

And by 2005, according to one forecast, this will grow to a billion.[15] Many European countries are no more than two to three years behind the United States in terms of Internet penetration, and the Scandinavian countries are ahead.[16]

Underlying the spread of connectivity and of electronic intelligence is the extraordinary force of Moore's Law: the observation first made by Gordon Moore, then chairman of Intel, that every eighteen months it is possible to double the number of transistor circuits etched on a computer chip. This law, or its equivalent, has prevailed for the past fifty years.[17] In the judgment of some of the world's leading experts, it is likely to prevail for the next fifty years.[18] Moore's Law implies a tenfold increase in memory and processing power every five years, a hundredfold every ten years, a thousandfold every fifteen. This is the most dramatic rate of sustained technical progress in history.[19]

This advance has pulled through extraordinary rates of associated innovation. Beginning only recently, communications capacity is exploding at a rate that dwarfs even Moore's Law. Improvements in data compression, amplification, and mutiplexing now permit a single fiber-optic strand to carry twenty-five terabits of information per second: twenty-five times more information than the average traffic load of all the world's communications networks put together. In the United States, communications companies are now laying optical fiber networks at the rate of 4,000 strand miles per day. The total bandwidth of U.S. communications systems is tripling every year.[20]

This tidal wave of universal connectivity is melting the glue bonding economic activities together. And it will separate, as nothing has separated before, the flow of information from the flow of physical things, allowing each to follow its own economics.

The Economics of Information and the Economics of Things

The pure economics of a physical "thing" and the pure economics of a piece of information are fundamentally different.[21] When a thing is sold, the seller ceases to own it; when an idea, a tune, or a blueprint is sold, the seller still possesses it and could possibly sell it again. Information can be replicated at almost zero cost without limit; things can be replicated only through the expense of manufacture. Things wear out: their performance deteriorates with wear and tear; information never wears out, although it can become unfashionable, obsolete, or simply untrue. A thing exists in a location and therefore a unique legal jurisdiction; information (as would-be censors and tax authorities are discovering) is nowhere and everywhere.

Some things are subject to diminishing returns: doubling farm labor does not double the output from the land. Some things are subject to increasing returns: big factories have lower unit costs than small factories. Information has *perfectly* increasing returns: spend the money to learn something once, and that knowledge can be reused at zero additional cost forever; double the number of uses and the cost per use halves.

The economics of things is consistent with efficient markets: fields and factories can compete against each other as price takers in competitive markets. The economics of information *requires* imperfect markets: unless the originators of information have some ability to limit the access of others to it (through copyright, or patent, or simple secrecy), they will never earn a return to justify the original investment. If there is no limit on the ability of others to copy it, owning information is worthless; if there is a limit, it is a monopoly. Either way, information does not behave like fields or factories.

The economics of physical things and the economics of pure information are thus fundamentally and qualitatively different. But as long as information is embedded within a physical thing, the two kinds of economics are wedded together: each is prevented from following its "pure" logic by the bond tying it to the other.

But their weightings have shifted. Over the centuries, the economics of information has steadily become less tied to the economics of things, as less physically intensive media have developed for the delivery of information. In the days before widespread literacy (to take a fanciful example), the stained-glass windows, altarpieces, and sculptures of a Gothic cathedral constituted an enormously capital-intensive medium for communicating information. Information did not come to people; people had to go to the information. The bundle of the physical and the informational was so overwhelmingly weighed down by the former that the economics of the latter was irrelevant: nobody saw fit to copyright a cathedral.[22]

When technology advanced in the form of literacy and printing, however, books could communicate much the same narrative through a far less capital-intensive means. Books still had their own physically defined costs of printing, binding, inventory, and distribution, but these were far lower than the cost of a pilgrimage to Canterbury. And issues of copyright and plagiarism appeared.

The advent of broadcasting permitted communication that is largely independent of the economics of things, but constrained to be one-way and monolithic. Telephone and fax have similarly freed certain kinds of communication and collaboration from the economics of things. But these media are limited by their narrow bandwidth.

Digital networks finally make it possible to blow up the link between rich information and its physical carrier. The Internet stands in the same relation to television as did television to books, and books to stained-glass windows.[23] The traditional link—between the medium and the message, between the flow of product-related information and the product itself, between the informational value chain and the physical value chain, between the economics of information and the economics of things—is broken.

Releasing Value

The economics of information and the economics of things have been tied together like participants in a three-legged race. Every business is consequently a compromise between the economics of information and the economics of things. Separating them breaks their mutual compromise and potentially releases enormous economic value.

Consider shelf space in a shop. Shelf space serves two different functions simultaneously. It is a *billboard* (information) that tells customers what they need to know in order to make a selection. It is also *inventory* (a thing)—the stock of goods residing between factory and consumer.

If retailers chose to lay out shelves for purely informational purposes, they would *maximize* the display—the bigger the shelf, the richer the choice presented to the consumer. If retailers focused on physical economics, however, they would *minimize* the display, to control the cost of inventory. But it is impossible to maximize and minimize simultaneously. So any retailer has to make a compromise between the economics of information, the billboard, and the economics of things, the inventory. Different shops make this

Frequently Asked Questions

1. **How can I tell if my business will be affected by the shifting economics of information?**

    Look at how and where information is a component of value in your current value chain. Map the flows of information through the value chain. Look at where compromises are created by the intertwining of the physical and the informational. The larger the value potential released by breaking these embedded compromises, the more susceptible will be your business to the shifting economics of information.

2. **What causes the breaking of the embedded compromises between information and things?**

    When information is carried by things—by a salesperson or by a piece of direct mail, for example—it goes where the things go and no further. It is constrained to follow the linear flow of the physical value chain. But once everyone is connected electronically, information can travel by itself. The traditional link between the flow of product-related information and the flow of the product itself, between the economics of information and the economics of things, can be broken. What is truly revolutionary about the explosion in connectivity is the possibility it offers to unbundle information from its physical carrier.

compromise in very different ways. High-end retailers focus more on the economics of presentation. Discount retailers compete more on the economics of inventory.

This compromise is ubiquitous. A newspaper publisher balances the demands of the paper's physical franchise, defined by the economics of its printing presses and trucking routes, with those of its informational franchise, defined by the universe of readers and advertisers interested in the content and readership that the newspaper delivers. Organizations balance the physical economics of location (it is more cost-effective to communicate over the telephone than to meet in person) against the informational economics of co-location (the informational exchange is richer if co-workers are meeting in the same place).

This compromise between the economics of information and the economics of things suppresses economic value, but more so in some businesses than in others. In grocery retailing, the value of the product is low, inventory turns are high, and the premium placed on selection by the customer (beyond some threshold) is comparatively low. The compromise between selection and inventory is not too severe. In book retailing, however, the value of the product is high, inventory turns are very low, and the premium on selection is much higher.[24] The informational imperative to carry high inventory and the logistical imperative to minimize it exist in strong tension with each other: lots of economic value is suppressed. *Separating* the economics of things from the economics of information—allowing for electronic search independent of warehouse delivery—therefore releases far more value in book selling than it does in grocery retailing.[25]

The implications of unraveling the informational value chain and the physical value chain—and then allowing each to evolve in accordance with its very distinct economics—are profound. Traditional business models will become deeply vulnerable wherever the compromise between the two sets of economics suppresses value. The separation will offer opportunities for companies to capitalize on *either* the liberated economics of information or the liberated economics of things. But none of the emergent business models needs to bear much resemblance to its antecedent.

Information, in short, may be the *end product* of only a minority of businesses, but it glues together value chains, supply chains, consumer franchises, and organizations across the entire economy. And it accounts for a grossly disproportionate share of competitive advantage and therefore of profits. The advent of rich connectivity and information standards, as we will discuss in greater detail in chapter 3, melts the informational glue that binds activities and participants together. It also allows an informational value chain to separate from the physical chain. Since the economics of information and the economics of physical things are fundamentally different, this can release tremendous economic value: value that was suppressed by their mutual compromise.

For the custodian of any established business, this has disturbing implications. It suggests that a "business" may no longer exist: the component pieces may separate as the informational glue bonding them together melts. It suggests that the informational and physical activities could unravel and indeed could fly apart because their underlying economics are so different. It suggests that some competitor could focus on a vulnerable sliver of the current value chain, where the incumbent is competitively disadvantaged or where the incumbent makes all its profit, and could appropriate just that piece. It suggests that all the incumbent's confidence about business definition, competitor threats, and competitive advantage—grounded doubtless in decades of competitive success—may be no more justified than it was for Britannica.

SOUND BITS

- Every business is an information business.

- Information is the glue that holds value chains, supply chains, consumer franchises, and organizations together. That glue is melting.

- Information accounts for the preponderance of competitive advantage and therefore profitability.

- The economics of information is quite different from the economics of physical things. In the majority of businesses the two are tied together in a mutually compromised bundle. That bundle is becoming obsolete.

- The vulnerability of a business is proportional to the extent of its embedded compromises: between different activities tied together by information flows, and between its economics of information and its economics of things.

3

RICHNESS AND REACH

tO THE EXTENT THAT INFORMATION is embedded in physical modes of delivery, a basic law governs its economics: *there is a universal trade-off between richness and reach*. But unbundle information from its physical carrier, and the richness/reach trade-off can blow up.[1]

The trade-off is fairly simple. "Richness" means the quality of information, as defined by the user: accuracy, bandwidth, currency, customization, interactivity, relevance, security, and so forth. The precise meaning of richness varies from one context to another, but in any one context, it is generally clear what the word means. "Reach" means the number of people who participate in the sharing of that information. (See the box titled "The Definitions of Richness and Reach.")

Until recently, it has been possible to share extremely rich information with a very small number of people and less rich information with a larger number, but it has been impossible to share simultaneously as much richness and

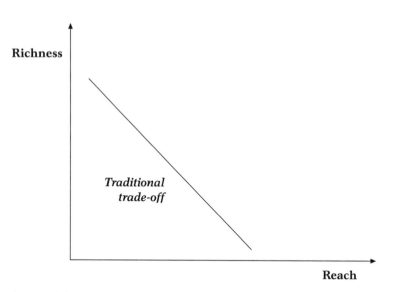

Source: Philip B. Evans and Thomas S. Wurster, "Strategy and the New Economics of Information," *Harvard Business Review,* September–October 1997, p. 74.

Figure 3-1: The Trade-off between Richness and Reach

reach as one would like. This trade-off is at the heart of the *old* economics of information (see Figure 3-1).

Communicating rich information has required proximity (people working in the same physical location) or dedicated channels (such as proprietary computer networks, retail stores, or a sales force). The costs or physical constraints of these channels, however, have limited the number of people who can access the information. Conversely, communicating information to a large audience has required compromises in the quality of that information. Technologies have not allowed us to achieve simultaneously as much richness and reach as we would like.[2]

Consider, for example, the alternative information channels through which sellers persuade buyers. Newspaper advertisements reach a wide range of possible customers

The Definitions of Richness and Reach

Reach is easy to understand. It simply means the number of people—at home or at work—exchanging information. The definition of richness of information is a bit more complex. It concerns six aspects of information:

- Bandwidth, or the amount of information that can be moved from sender to receiver in a given time: stock quotes are narrowband; a feature film is broadband.

- The degree to which the information can be customized: an advertisement on television is far less customized than a personal sales pitch but reaches many more people.

- Interactivity: dialogue is possible for a small group, but to reach millions the message must be a monologue.

- Reliability: information is reliable when exchanged among a small group of trusted individuals but is not when it is circulating among a large group of strangers.

- Security: managers share highly sensitive business information only in closed-door meetings, but they will disseminate less sensitive information to a wider audience.

- Currency: on Wall Street, where seconds count, a few market makers have instantaneous quotes, a larger group of financial institutions receives quotes with a three- to fifteen-minute delay, and most retail investors receive quotes with at least a 15-minute delay.

with limited, static content. Direct mail and telemarketing are a bit richer in customization and interactivity, but much more expensive, and therefore have to be targeted. Relative to advertisers, direct marketers give up reach in order to add richness. A salesman giving his pitch offers the highest level of personalization, dialogue, and empathy, but with only one customer at a time. The marketing mix is thus the apportionment of information resources across a trade-off between richness and reach.

Buyers live with, and adapt to, the same trade-off. It forces them to search hierarchically. They have to navigate their way from high-reach/low-richness information sources (such as the phone book, which offers only contact information but reaches a wide universe of sellers) to high-richness/low-reach sources (such as the salesman, who offers to a single customer richly detailed, interactive, and personalized information about his own limited range of wares). For consumers, brand knowledge is simply a high-richness/low-reach stock of information that short-circuits the laborious task of hierarchical search.

Supply chains exhibit the same trade-off. When companies conduct business with one another, the number of parties they deal with is inversely proportional to the richness of the information they need to exchange.

Citibank's currency traders source euros and yen from hundreds of institutions, precisely because the informational richness needed to support currency trading amounts to just two numbers: quantity and price. Currency traders do not need to build relationships or swap favors, even with their colleagues at the next desk: the information requirements of the business put a far higher premium on reach than they do on most kinds of informational richness.

Conversely, Toyota and Wal-Mart have narrowed their reach by moving to fewer and larger long-term supplier contracts to allow a richer coordination of marketing and logistics (see Figure 3-2). They built sophisticated systems for electronic data interchange (EDI) with their suppliers, but the enormous cost of custom installation to bring supply sys-

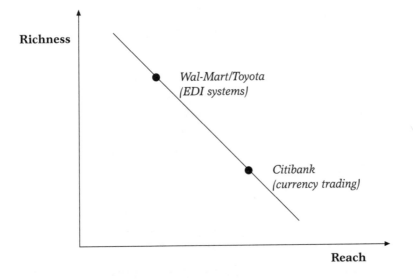

Figure 3-2: Positioning on the Richness/Reach Trade-off: Wal-Mart, Toyota, and Citibank

tems into mutual compatibility forced these companies to narrow their sourcing to the largest and most capable vendors. Japanese manufacturers became well known in the 1980s for deliberately narrowing their supply base in this fashion and then closely collaborating with their suppliers to maximize quality and minimize inventory and delivery time. They gained richness at the sacrifice of reach.

The array of sourcing strategies, with Citibank at one extreme and Toyota and Wal-Mart at the other, reflects the trade-off between richness and reach. More generally, the hierarchical structure of supply chains, in which each participant deals only with its immediate suppliers and its immediate customers, reflects another aspect of the trade-off: it is too difficult and too expensive for everyone to have rich and directly collaborative relations with everyone else in an industry.[3]

Organizations support rich information exchange among their limited group of employees or members, whereas markets trade in less rich information among a wider universe. The boundary of the corporation is thus a point on the trade-off between richness and reach.

Within a corporation, traditional concepts of span of control and hierarchical reporting are predicated on the fact that communication cannot be rich and broad reaching simultaneously. Jobs are structured to channel rich communication among a few people standing in a hierarchical relationship to one another (upward or downward), and broader communication is effected through the indirect routes of the organizational pyramid.

"Relationships," among and within corporations, as well as with retail customers; "loyalty" to a product or an employer; and "trust" of a person or a brand are all the products of *rich* exchanges of information among people who by doing so have narrowed the *reach* of their options. The marketing mix, searching and switching behavior, branding, retail franchises, supply chain relationships, organization—indeed even the boundaries of the corporation—all are built on this pervasive, universal, and obvious trade-off between richness and reach.

Asymmetries of Information

In all these contexts, the trade-off between richness and reach generates *asymmetries of information:* differences in knowledge among people or companies that affect their bargaining power. Someone selling a used car knows more about its faults than does the buyer. The buyer may protect himself by hiring a mechanic to look it over or by offering less than the car appears to be worth. If the car is actually in good condition, the seller suffers from the asymmetry as much as the buyer, since she has no way to convince the buyer that her affection for the vehicle is genuine.

Some asymmetries (such as those relating to personal likes and dislikes) are inevitable, but many arise from the richness/reach trade-off. Somebody, somewhere, has useful objective information, but the parties do not have free and equal access to it. There may be no third party who is better informed about a secondhand car than the owner, but J.D. Power has excellent data on customer satisfaction, the Kelly Blue Book lists the prevailing wholesale and retail prices, and the mechanic who serviced the car keeps its maintenance records. But if only one party (such as a professional car dealer) has access to some of this information, he will use it to exploit the other's ignorance. And if neither party has the information, they may fail, out of mutual mistrust, to make a deal. Asymmetries of information impose substantial costs on the disadvantaged participant in a transaction, and often on the advantaged as well.

This is true in general. The trade-off between richness and reach is based on the existence of information channels: physical infrastructures or behavioral patterns that support limited movements of information. But the existence of channels implies that some have privileged access and others do not: channels imply asymmetries. Some can get rich information only through an intermediary who has access to the channel and who extracts the value of his informational chokehold. Eliminate the richness/reach trade-off, make the channel universally accessible, and the asymmetry collapses.

And that is precisely what is beginning to happen. Digital networks are now making it possible for a very large number of people to exchange very rich information. The richness/reach trade-off is being displaced and, in some cases, obliterated. Once information can travel by itself and there are standards that allow everyone to share that information, it becomes possible to have richness *and* reach. This blowup of the trade-off between richness and reach is creating a *new* economics of information. And with the blowup go the behavioral patterns, institutions, and asymmetries that have defined marketing, supply chains, organization, and the boundaries of the corporation.

The Explosion in Connectivity and the Advent of Universal Standards

Two forces drive this displacement: the explosion of connectivity and the adoption of common information standards. As we discussed in chapter 2, the growth rate of connectivity has been exceeding almost every prediction. Electronic networks allow information to flow largely independently of the economics of things. Liberated from the constraint of a physical carrier, information can flow with negligible cost of delivery, customization, or delay. Connectivity alone, however, is not sufficient to break the trade-off between richness and reach. The second requirement is common standards. The rapid emergence of universal technical standards for communication, which allows everybody to communicate with everybody else at essentially zero cost, constitutes a sea change. In many ways, this development is the more profound of the two transformations taking place (see Figure 3-3).

As long as electronic channels are proprietary, they limit reach: users can get richness only by restricting reach to the closed group of network participants. However, proprietary electronic networks are giving way to open ones. Commercial e-mail systems are now largely interoperable, as each has adopted the common transmission and presentation protocols of the Internet. Proprietary EDI systems are being

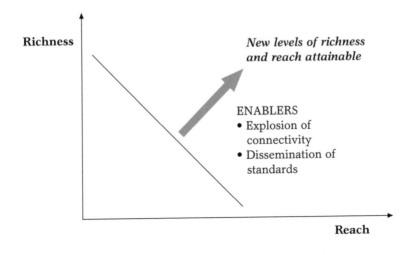

Figure 3-3: The Blowup of the Richness/Reach Trade-off

supplanted by industry-wide extranets, such as ANX in the automotive industry, which share a common set of communication standards. On-line services, originally conceived as closed, proprietary services, have opened Internet access for their members. Within the corporation, functional information "silos" are being replaced by intranets, initially for the static presentation of reference information (knowledge management systems, HR data, and so forth) but prospectively for increasingly mission-critical applications.

However, the shift in standards is not just from proprietary to open. The Internet, extranets, and intranets are all variants on exactly the same thing.[4] They use a set of lowest common denominator technical standards. These triumph because of the principle of "good enough": at some point in the advance of a technology, generic standards become good enough for their advantages in universal acceptance to outweigh their disadvantages in any specific application.

The logic of "good enough" is illustrated by the way the general-purpose PC replaced such dedicated devices as the word processor, adding machine, and Rolodex. In the early days, dedicated devices (usually integrating hardware and software) were necessary to make office technologies work. At some point in the early 1980s, however, the fact that a PC could also run e-mail and spreadsheets came to outweigh the still superior speed and keyboard layout of a word processor. Over time, processing speeds increased and the PC's lack of dedicated hardware became less and less noticeable. As the PC market skyrocketed, suppliers reaped the benefits of the experience curve, competition intensified and prices plummeted. Eventually, because of the tremendous growth of the market, better word processing software was being written for the PC than for any proprietary word processing system. The dedicated word processor went the way of Quotron terminals, high-end calculators, and analog computers— defeated first on reach, but eventually on richness as well. The lowest common denominator across a range of uses had simply become, for most purposes, *good enough.*

Over just the past five years, lowest-common-denominator standards have swept the board for static, textual information where security and speed are not critical (e.g., HTML as a standard for presenting text). Over the next ten years, many other types of information will succumb to the same principle: mission-critical, higher-volume applications, collaborative and distributed processing, confidential data, voice, full-screen, high-definition audio and video entertainment. There are no fundamental technical barriers to building standards because memory and processing power continue to be driven by Moore's Law and bandwidth is exploding. For some applications, there is legitimate argument over *when.* There can be no real argument over *whether.*

From Technical Standards to Content Standards

Each time universal standards have emerged throughout history, the consequences have been dramatic. Railroads are an obvious example. In the industry's early days, railway companies operated their tracks with different gauges, making it necessary to transship goods from one railcar to another in order to get them across the country. In the 1880s, the railway companies adopted a standard gauge nationwide and in so doing blew up the previous limitations of reach.[5] The standard allowed goods to be shipped nonstop across the country. The emergence of dial tone and other common policies, procedures, and standards had a similar impact in allowing long-distance telephony. And the adoption of AC power and the standard electric power plug was vital to the growth of the consumer appliance industry.

If universal and open standards today were created only for transporting data, this would be dramatic enough, comparable to rail widths and dial tone. However, in the digital world (unlike railways, unlike telephones), *there is no qualitative difference between transportation standards and content standards,* and there is a natural evolution from one into the other.

IP (Internet protocol), for example, is a standard that routes packages of information around a network. Other standards build on this capability. TCP adds verification to IP. HTTP aggregates TCP/IP "packets" of information into documents. HTML formats the HTTP documents into Web pages. XML formats these documents into a wider set of self-describing files. HL7 is a content standard that uses XML to record medical information. Digital standards cumulate, starting with transportation and ending with content.

This is very different from analog electronic technologies. With analog technologies, there is a qualitative barrier between the standards for transmitting information and the standards (if any) for the content being transmitted. The formats and protocols for a fax machine (transmission) and for the document being faxed (content) have no relation to each other. Dial tone has nothing to do with the content of phone conversations. But when content is digital, there is no such barrier. Standards established at one level can serve as the basis for standards at a higher level.

The mathematician John von Neumann first articulated this insight when he described the EDVAC computer project in 1945. Von Neumann conceived that a digital computer could store and retrieve *instructions* in exactly the same way that it stores and retrieves *data*. Instructions could therefore serve as the raw material for other instructions, programs could read and write programs, higher-level languages could build on lower-level languages, and hardwired functions would therefore be the starting point, not the endpoint, of a machine's capabilities. Von Neumann was the first to recognize how this unique characteristic of the stored-program computer would enable a then-inconceivable degree of sophistication and adaptability.[6]

Von Neumann's original vision is playing out, not just in computer design, but also in the self-organization of a global network of people and institutions. And that is qualitatively new.

Critical Mass

There is nothing that guarantees that higher-order standards will emerge out of lower-order standards: it is just a possibility. But there is every reason why such standards will be attempted and why enormous resources will be devoted to driving their penetration.

Standards are characterized by a snowball effect: the greater the number of people using them, the more valuable they become, and therefore the greater the number of people motivated to use them. The classic, almost comic, example is the QWERTY typewriter keyboard. It was originally designed to make typing as *difficult* as possible, because old typewriters were so slow in retracting keys from the page that if people typed too quickly, the mechanism jammed. People learned the keyboard layout they found on the machine, and manufacturers made the layout that people used. A century later, we are still using a standard that was designed to be as bad as possible—even though the technology has improved and our typing mechanisms no longer jam.

As this example illustrates, standards are subject to increasing returns and a powerful "network" effect: the greater their penetration, the greater their competitive advantage.[7] In many contexts, this has resulted in room for only one standard worldwide (e.g., VHS, for consumer videotapes). Whoever owns that standard, even if only in the most indirect of ways, has the opportunity to extract enormous value. This creates a strong incentive to invest in creating such a standard, to ally with others to increase the chance of acceptance, and if necessary, to give away 99 percent of its proprietary content to capitalize on the sliver of advantage that remains.

There is no guarantee that any particular content-related standard will be feasible, although Moore's Law makes it ten times easier every five years. There is no guarantee that the right alliance of players will achieve critical mass and drive their standard to become a global norm, although these players have the resources, the intelligence, and a clear understanding of the value of the endgame. There is no guarantee that any particular standard will succeed, and indeed many have failed. But the global reach that existing lower-level standards have already achieved, the extraordinary value that higher-level standards can therefore release, and the financial rewards that accrue to whoever establishes them first all indicate that the process of cumulative standard building has passed a critical threshold.

Blowing Up the Trade-off between Richness and Reach

It is connectivity and standards together that displace the trade-off between richness and reach. They allow advising, alerting, authenticating, bidding, collaborating, comparing, informing, searching, specifying, and switching, with a richness that is constrained only by the underlying standards and a reach that is constrained only by the number of players connected and using that standard.

For example, OFX is a standard, developed by Intuit, Microsoft, and others, for the presentation of personal financial information. As it evolves into a comprehensive standard, it will allow an individual to specify a financial need, receive and compare bids, incorporate data or advice from any source that she trusts, apply systematic selection criteria, execute transactions, automate routine tasks, and integrate her financial statements, all *while dealing with an essentially unlimited number of institutions*. Ordinary individuals can exercise the purchasing sophistication of professionals. The comprehensive financial planning previously available only to private banking clients becomes available to all. The seamless integration previously achieved only by putting all one's business with a single institution is now available across multiple accounts. The customer enjoys both richness *and* reach.

As the trade-off between richness and reach blows up, economic relationships, in all their manifestations, will change radically. A sales force, a system of branches, a printing press, a chain of stores, or a delivery fleet—which once served as formidable barriers to entry because they took years and heavy investment to build—will suddenly become expensive liabilities. New competitors will come from nowhere to steal customers. Similarly, the replacement of expensive, proprietary, legacy systems with inexpensive, open extranets will make it easier for companies to bid for supply contracts, join a virtual factory, or form a competing supply chain. Inside large corporations, the emergence of universal, open standards for exchanging information over intranets will foster cross-functional teams and will accelerate the demise of hierarchical structures and their proprietary information systems.

When everyone can exchange rich information without constraints on reach, the channel choices for marketers, the inefficiencies of consumer search, the hierarchical structure of supply chains, the organizational pyramid, asymmetries of information, and the boundaries of the corporation itself will all be thrown into question. The competitive advantages that depended on them will be challenged. The business structures that had been shaped by them will fall apart.

We call this process of transformation *deconstruction*. Over the next five to ten years, many relationships throughout the business world will deconstruct. It is already beginning to happen.

SOUND BITS

- Over decades, Moore's Law has been a driver in three successive agendas for management: the first was high-volume data processing, the second was decentralized networking, and the third will be the blowup of the trade-off between richness and reach.

- The trade-off between richness and reach is the informational foundation on which relationships, consumer franchises, vertical integration, horizontal integration, and asymmetries of information are largely based.

- Shifting the trade-off between richness and reach melts the informational glue that bonds business relationships. It "deconstructs" value chains, supply chains, franchises, and organizations.

- The blowup is driven by connectivity, by the triumph of "good enough" communication standards, and by migration of those standards into the organization and presentation of content.

- There is nothing inevitable about the evolution of standards. But the global value of even tangential ownership, the low cost of creating them, the ease of forming alliances to push them, and the extraordinary jackpot that they occasionally offer will all motivate smart and well-financed players to try to establish standards.

4

DECONSTRUCTION

DECONSTRUCTION" IS THE DISMANTLING and reformulation of traditional business structures. It results from two forces: the separation of the economics of information from the economics of things, and the blowup (*within* the economics of information) of the trade-off between richness and reach. Traditional business structures include value chains, supply chains, organizations, and consumer franchises. When the trade-off between richness and reach is blown up, there is no longer a need for the components of these business structures to be integrated. The new economics of information blows all these structures to bits. The pieces will then recombine into new business structures, based on the separate economics of information and things.

Newspapers

Consider the newspaper business. It has a vertically and horizontally integrated value chain. Journalists and advertisers supply copy, editors and subeditors lay it out, the press prints the physical product, and an elaborate distribution system delivers it to readers each morning. Newspapers exist, and can survive and profit as intermediaries between journalists and readers, because of the economies of scale in the printing press. Writers cannot reach readers directly because they cannot cheaply print and distribute their work alone. Given its economies of scale, it makes sense for the newspaper to bundle multiple news services together, and it makes further sense to add in all the other material that benefits from the same method of reproduction and distribution: classifieds, display advertisements, inserts, stock quotes, features, cartoons, TV listings, and so forth. These products cross-subsidize each other: some pull in particular segments of readers, others pull in particular segments of advertisers. All contribute to the overall fixed costs of production and distribution.

Gurus have been forecasting for years the possibility of a high-resolution electronic "tablet" newspaper, which would be loaded with daily content over the phone line, support full-motion video, offer all the advantages of electronic intelligence, and cost less per day than the price of a paper newspaper.[1] Like the equally famous "paperless office," it has not happened yet, and is not likely to become popular in the foreseeable future. As newspaper executives point out, the broadsheet is an extraordinarily cheap, convenient, and user-friendly way to distribute information. Electronic tablets are not going to replace it very soon.

However, that response is to misunderstand the nature of the challenge facing newspapers: it assumes that the transformation of the business is an all-or-nothing proposition. The question is not whether and when newspapers will go electronic. The question is more basic: will newspapers still remain a vertically and horizontally integrated business?

Deconstruction posits a melting of the glue that binds the newspaper value chain together. The glue in this case is the economics of things—printing presses and distribution—tying together the informational content. Once other means of distribution become possible, *the bundle can no longer be taken for granted.*

Liberated from the economics of things, journalists will be able to e-mail content directly to readers. Readers will be able to mix and match content from an unlimited number of sources. They will be able to download news daily (or several times a day) from multiple news services. They will be able to obtain movie reviews, travel features, and recipes directly from magazines, book publishers, and master chefs. Star columnists, cartoonists, or the U.S. Weather Service can send their content directly to subscribers. Intermediaries—Internet portals, intelligent agents, formatting software, or, for that matter, editorial teams—can format and package content to meet readers' individual interests. The "daily us" of the traditional newspaper could be replaced by a customized "daily me."[2]

Almost all these things are already happening. On-line journalism is burgeoning. Most traditional newspaper content is available somewhere on the Web. Portals offer quite sophisticated customization of home pages, including on-line tracking of an investment portfolio, continuous weather updates, local entertainment listings, and alerts on topics of special interest. But still, convenient and nifty as these services are, there is little evidence that they are drawing readers away from the daily newspaper.

However, deconstruction does not have to occur—indeed rarely will occur—across the board. Deconstruction does not mean that the newspaper business as a whole is vulnerable, but rather that the critical pieces of the business are vulnerable.

Classified advertising is a natural on-line product. When posted and accessed electronically, classified advertisers can offer continuously updated listings, extensive text and pictures, prospectively even video clips. Buyers can search systematically by whatever criteria they choose, set alerts, access related information, and respond via e-mail. The inconvenience of booting a computer is a minor consideration when selling a car or buying a house.

The migration of classified advertising has a compelling logic and is already well under way.[3] However, classifieds account for about 40 percent of the revenues of the typical newspaper but only 10 percent of its costs. The 30 percent contribution from classifieds is well in excess of the margin of just about every newspaper in the United States. If classifieds were lost, most newspapers would become financially unsustainable. *That* is the threat of deconstruction. Not electronic tablets, not Yahoo! providing a customized Daily Me, but the loss of classifieds. Deconstruction is most likely to strike in precisely that sliver of the value chain where the incumbent can least afford to let it happen.

Newspapers are fighting back. They have moved aggressively into the electronic classified business. They have exploited their advantage as incumbents in print to provide an integrated print and electronic classified offering that reaches the widest population of buyers and sellers. And because they currently own the biggest classified "marketplace," bringing together the largest number of buyers and sellers, they are well positioned to translate their dominance of the old business into dominance of the new.

But how much is that marketplace advantage worth? Can newspapers price electronic classifieds at the same rates they charge for print? Viewed as a stand-alone business, they are charging $40 in revenues for every $10 in costs, a 75 percent operating margin. (The only reason they are able to get away with that kind of pricing is that it *isn't* a stand-alone business.) Can they get away with that kind of pricing when there are no barriers to entry, and when costs, incidentally, have dropped by a factor of over half? If newspapers preserve their price level, they risk ceding the marketplace to an electronic-only competitor who is less greedy. If they give up enough of the margin to keep the business, they lose the cash flow that supports the economics of the print product.

Either way, the subsidy that supports the print product plummets. The print business is then caught between reduced revenues and its high level of fixed costs. Newspapers cut content or raise subscription and newsstand prices, which drives down readership. Readership losses drive down the price that display advertisers are willing to pay. The loss of reader and advertiser revenues in turn necessitates further cost cutting. This downward spiral then creates opportunities for focused competitors to pick off other parts of the value chain: second-order deconstructions that would not have been economic otherwise. So the greatest threat to newspapers is not the total substitution of a new business model, but steady erosion of the business through a sequence of partial substitutions.

This does not mean the demise of newspapers. There is a powerful rationale for a bundle of news and commentary, something to do with editorial voice, shared daily experience, brand, authority, and the reader's simple desire to be surprised by the unexpected. And people are clearly willing to pay for it: the actual cost of editorial content today is about equal to the average price of a subscription. After the deconstruction of the old bundle, which was shaped by the shared economics of presses and distribution, we will see the rise of a new bundle (or new bundles; there is no reason to presume only one solution) that will reflect the liberated economics of information.

Retail Banking

Retail banking will undergo similar deconstruction. Today's business model is a vertically and horizontally integrated value chain: multiple products are originated, packaged, sold, and cross-sold through a common set of proprietary distribution channels. These channels have high fixed costs and substantial economies of utilization and scale. These factors determine the rules of engagement and competitive advantage. The fundamental unit of value is the customer relationship. Distribution systems are optimized around servicing that relationship. Some products are sold at low or negative margins in order to acquire and build relationships. Others are then cross-sold at high margins to extract value from relationships that have been established. All contribute to the common costs of an integrated distribution system.

Electronic home banking looks at first glance like another, but cheaper, distribution channel: the banker's equivalent of the tablet newspaper. Many banks see it that way, hoping that widespread adoption of home banking might enable them to scale down their high-cost physical channels. Many offer proprietary software to support home banking and even free electronic transactions. But electronic home banking is much more than the emergence of a new distribution channel for incumbents. Customers now can access information and make transactions in a variety of fundamentally new ways.

One way is through personal financial software. At the time of writing, some twelve million households in the United States regularly use financial management software, such as Intuit's Quicken or Microsoft Money, to manage their checkbooks and integrate their personal financial affairs. Current versions of these programs use modems to access electronic switches operated by CheckFree or Integrion, which, in turn, route instructions or queries to the consumer's own bank. Customers can then pay bills, make transfers, receive electronic statements, reconcile their checkbooks, and integrate account data into their personal financial plans. Bankers do not like this: they cannot brand or control what the customer sees on the screen, and it is a general principle of strategy not to let companies like Intuit of Microsoft get between oneself and one's customers. But customers are still largely locked into dealing with their own bank, albeit by a nonproprietary route.

However, there is yet another way. Most major financial institutions maintain Web sites, which can be accessed using a browser. Until recently, the Web sites of financial institutions offered only very basic information: product and service descriptions, the annual report, and points of contact. But the consumer could reach thousands of such sites with equal ease.

This presented the consumer with a trade-off between richness and reach: either rich services (via proprietary software or Quicken) from one's own bank, or very limited offerings from a wide-reaching universe of institutions (via the Web). However, *this trade-off is entirely artificial.* Once connectivity has been established there is every incentive for players to create *standards* that migrate up from the transportation layer into content, standards that allow for increasing richness across the entire universe of institutions. And that is precisely what is happening.

SSL, SET, and other encryption standards have largely solved the problem of security. Microsoft and Intuit (driven in part by the loss of momentum in their old desktop-based concept) are pursuing strategies of converting their products into "value-added browsers," able seamlessly to draw information from the Web and integrate it on the desktop. Quicken file formats have become the de facto standard for the presentation of statement information over the Web. A more comprehensive set of standards, called OFX, has been agreed to by the major players, supporting Web-based statements, payments, transfers, and queries. Future versions of OFX will support the presentation of bills, brokerage transactions, and the soliciting and comparison of bids for retail products and services. Bridges between personal financial software and the Web sites of financial institutions, combined with advances in reliability, security, digital signatures, and legally binding electronic contracts, will enable the Web to support the full range of banking services.

When that happens, the trade-off between richness and reach in retail banking will be broken. Customers will be able to contact *any* financial institution for *any* kind of service or information. They will be able to maintain a balance sheet on their desktop, drawing on data from multiple institutions. They will be able to compare alternative product offerings and sweep funds automatically between accounts at different institutions. They will be able to announce their product requirements and accept bids. They will be able to make sophisticated comparisons between product and service offerings.

The sheer breadth of choice will create the need for third parties to play the role of navigator or facilitating agent. Some companies will create (or make available) databases on interest rates, risk ratings, and service histories. Others will create insurance and mortgage calculators or intelligent-agent software that can search for and evaluate product offerings. Still others will authenticate the identity of counterparts or serve as guarantors of performance, confidentiality, or creditworthiness (see Figure 4-1).

Moreover, the greatest driver of home banking is yet to appear: electronic bill presentation. Once it becomes possible for bills to be e-mailed in standard format and paid at the press of a button, the productivity benefits to the consumer will become far more powerful than any retail banking service offered today. That "killer app" will drive usage, ancillary products, and deconstruction to higher levels of penetration.

The second-order consequences are profound. As it becomes easier for customers to compare and switch from one supplier to another, the value, indeed the meaning, of the primary banking relationship will become problematic. The competitive value of one-stop shopping and established relationships will drop. Cross-selling will become more difficult. Available information about the customer's behavior and preferences will become more evenly distributed among competing institutions. The winner in any contest for a consumer's business is less likely to be the primary bank and more likely to be whoever makes the best offer for that *particular* product or service. Competitive advantage will be determined product by product, and therefore providers with broad product lines will lose ground to focused specialists.

Distribution will be done by the phone or cable company, statements by personal financial management software, facilitation and navigation by different kinds of agent software, databases, and advisers, and origination by any number of different kinds of product specialists. The vertically and horizontally integrated value chain of retail banking will be deconstructed.

Deconstructed, but not destroyed. All the old functions

will still be performed, as well as some new ones. Banks will not become obsolete, but their current business definitions will—specifically, the concept that a bank is an integrated business where multiple products are originated, packaged, sold, and cross-sold through proprietary distribution channels. The smartest institutions will transform themselves

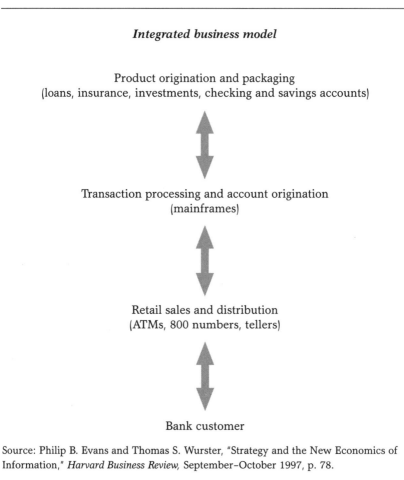

Integrated business model

Product origination and packaging
(loans, insurance, investments, checking and savings accounts)

Transaction processing and account origination
(mainframes)

Retail sales and distribution
(ATMs, 800 numbers, tellers)

Bank customer

Source: Philip B. Evans and Thomas S. Wurster, "Strategy and the New Economics of Information," *Harvard Business Review,* September–October 1997, p. 78.

Figure 4-1: The Deconstruction of Retail Financial Services: Some Illustrative Connections among Players

into navigators or into product specialists.

The deconstruction of the value chain in banking is not as distant and futuristic as many think. In fact it has already happened. Twenty years ago, corporate banking was a "spread" business—that is, banks made money by charging a higher interest rate for loans than they paid for deposits.

Reconfigured business model

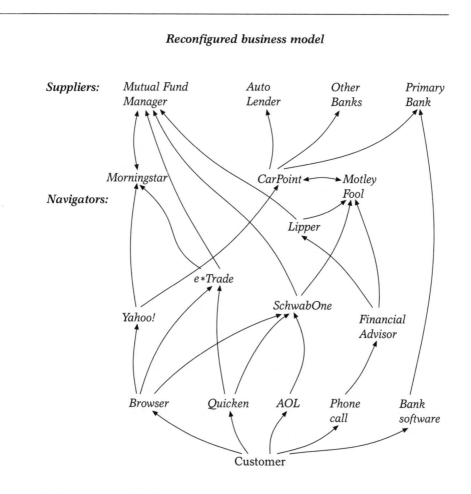

Their business model required them to form deep relationships with their corporate customers so that they could
pump deposits and loans through that distribution system.
Services were given away to lubricate the relationship. But
then, thanks to technology, corporate customers got access to
the same financial markets that the banks used: reach and
information symmetry transformed the relationship. Banks
were disintermediated. Credit now flows directly from ultimate lender to ultimate borrower through the capital markets, *facilitated and navigated* by bankers who rate the risk,
give advice, make markets, and serve as custodians.

Today, corporate banking consists of small businesses that
are largely stand-alone (even when they function under the
umbrella of a big bank), and compete product by product.
The bankers make money through the fees they charge for
these individual services, not from spread and cross-subsidy.
Clients no longer bundle their purchases; relationships are
more volatile and are different for each banking product.
Corporate banking was deconstructed by a shift in information technology that allowed corporations the same rich
access to the financial markets that the banks had. Deprived
of the role of privileged information channel, banks had to
switch to the roles of navigator, agent, and facilitator. Two
decades later, after a ten-thousandfold advance in the economics of information, we may be ready for the same logic
to work its way through the retail banking business.

Many bankers deny all this. They point out that consumers are not likely to put their checking account out to
frequent bid among banks merely because it becomes technically possible. The cost of switching accounts is still high.
True. However, the real cost of switching will be the cost of
switching personal financial software, so if anybody enjoys a
locked relationship with the consumer, it will be the soft-

ware vendor. Moreover, the bigger margins are in big-ticket items, where the logic of exploiting reach is most compelling. Consumers are most likely to change their behavior in precisely those products where the financial institution has the most margin to lose, because these are the same products for which consumers have the most to gain.[4]

Four Steps to Assessing Vulnerability

There are four critical steps to understanding how deconstruction will play out in individual industries.

- **First, examine how informational economics shape your industry.** What are the richness/reach trade-offs that have been made, and how do those trade-offs underpin existing business structures?

- **Second, consider how new technologies can shift these existing structures.** How will new technologies transform these trade-offs? How quickly will this occur? And in what sequence will they be transformed? What is the potential impact of that transformation on the current business model? How can informational and physical activities separate into new kinds of businesses?

- **Third, analyze how the various players in the business system could create economic value as a consequence of these changes.** In a world without the existing trade-off between richness and reach, how will the new economic forces rebalance, and what new economic opportunities will present themselves? When the business deconstructs into separate businesses, what kinds of competitive advantages will each successor business require to exploit the new opportunities? How will advantage and value be redistributed among the players?

- **Fourth, lead the transition from the old business model to the new one.** How can the business get from here to there? Jettisoning a successful existing strategy and creating a radically different one is an enormous challenge. But designing and then building the business model capable of executing that new strategy is even tougher.

Bankers also argue that only a minority of those consumers who own PCs use them for home banking. Also true (though less true each year). However, the profitability of retail banking relationships today is driven by assets, income, and number of transactions, and is very heavily skewed toward a minority of profitable customers. The users of personal financial management software, not surprisingly, tend to have above average wealth, income, and number of transactions. They are very profitable customers. In fact, the 12 percent of households that currently use personal financial management software in the United States account for about three-quarters of the profit of the banking system. So, as with classifieds in the newspaper, it does not require a very large switch in customer behavior for the fixed-cost economics of the retail bank to collapse. Again, the most valuable sliver of the business is the most likely target for deconstruction.[5]

Automotive Retailing

Car dealers are sitting ducks. Like newspapers, like retail banks, auto dealers perform a disparate bundle of informational and physical functions. They tell the customer about models and options. They offer test drives. They broker financing. They make a market in secondhand cars. They hold inventory, prepare cars for final delivery, and perform after-sales maintenance, often under warranty from the manufacturer.

These very different activities are bundled together because of the logic of one-stop shopping: consumers are nervous about their ability to get rid of their old car or get financing. They have few alternative sources of information about models and features. They want the manufacturer to stand behind the servicing. When they find their car, they want it right away. Combinations of these motives lead enough consumers to accept enough parts of the bundle to sustain the combined business definition.

This bundling has pricing implications. Once consumers have identified a chosen model, they tend to see price as the only selection criterion, and because this is a major and high-risk purchase, they shop around. This forces dealers to compete aggressively on price—so aggressively that most make little or no margin on the sale of the car itself. To offset this, they then extract high margins from the low-attention, ancillary products and services: options packages, financing, secondhand trade-in, and warranty. As with newspapers, as with banks, the logic of the bundle drives the practice of cross-subsidy.

Dealers have an information advantage over the customer. They know the going rate for a secondhand car, the true invoice cost, the pricing at other dealerships. Most customers don't. Dealers provide information that is biased toward the specific models or option configurations that they happen to have on the lot. Customers expend a lot of physical energy trying to correct these asymmetries, pitting one dealer against another. They then expend emotional energy on haggling. Everybody suffers: asymmetry of information drives up the consumer's cost of search and also increases the dealer's sales costs because so much time is wasted on unsuccessful sales pitches.

There are also compromises in the physical configuration of the dealer network. The ideal network for providing after-sales warranty service would consist of smaller repair shops close to the customer. But the ideal network for holding new-car inventory would be highly centralized: a handful of large regional sites. The actual dealership network is *local enough* to provide a reasonably convenient shopping experience for people who want to look at new cars. It is *regional enough* to provide reasonable efficiency in the management of inventory. But it is a compromise between the varying economics of its constituent activities.

The result is a massively compromised business system. As a physical distributor, it is less efficient than direct factory delivery or regional distribution centers. Its service levels are inferior to those of specialized repair chains. As a provider of unbiased product information its value added is negative. Its finance offerings are overpriced. As a market maker in used cars, it exploits the ignorance and anxiety of its customers. But as long as these activities are bundled together (by the customer's economics of searching), none of this matters: the only mainstream competition for an auto dealer is other auto dealers, who are just as bad.

However, eliminate the informational glue holding all these functions in a single, compromised business model, and the multiple businesses that emerge can evolve in radically different directions, each driven by its own, very different economics. It is easy to imagine an uncompromised business targeted against each function that the dealer performs.

Web sites provided by the car manufacturers, for example, make it easy for customers to compare the specifications of different cars. And although a manufacturer's marketing division is hardly an unbiased source of information, a large car company has far more brand exposure than a dealer, and will therefore represent its products more objectively. There are also independent third parties, such as *Consumer Reports* and J.D. Power, plus on-line brokers like AutoVantage, Car-Point, and Autobytel, all of whom provide objective model data in a standardized format and, in some cases, comparisons of competing models.

Since they track the information anyway, the manufacturers are also the most advantaged in providing data on model availability. Regional information on availability would enable the consumer to make trade-offs between the time of delivery and the cost of the car without having to contact every dealer in the state. The manufacturer could even offer the choice of having a car that is not locally available delivered in three weeks at a low cost or in two days at a higher cost.

The business of financing cars already exists quite independent of the dealer. When financing options are only a click away via Quicken, consumers can effortlessly contact hundreds of financial institutions for a car loan. Lenders assess two different types of information when deciding whether they will make a loan: the borrower's creditworthiness and the collateral value of the automobile being purchased. Standards already exist for presenting such information. So the necessary information can easily be disseminated to a wide range of financial institutions, which could then bid for the business. The convenience advantage of credit through the dealer largely evaporates. Moreover, the captive automotive credit companies could use credit to market their parents' product line far more effectively if they reached the consumer directly, instead of relying on the high-cost, inefficient, and frequently disloyal channel of the dealer.

If the informational functions in the business were performed separately, the physical logistics could then be structured to maximize efficiency. Inventories would be kept in much larger lots on a regional, rather than a local, basis, probably by the manufacturer. This centralized arrangement would enable improved inventory turns. Ultimately (and not too far into the future) manufacturers will be able to build most cars to order, largely getting rid of finished-goods inventory. Either way, the logical method to buy a new car becomes by direct purchase from the manufacturer.

The business of performing warranty service could also be transformed. The primary reason why customers take their car back to the dealer is that the manufacturer stands behind the dealer's performance. But that is merely a contractual arrangement. As the cost of contracting and monitoring falls, manufacturers could contract for warranty service with independent businesses or franchises of specialist automotive repair shops, certifying their quality levels to consumers. Such services would compete on local presence and would have no need to sign an exclusive arrangement with any one manufacturer. This would offer greater convenience, lower cost, and better-quality service.

In a deconstructed world, the secondhand car business would largely split into two stand-alone businesses: one for "old" used cars that are no longer under warranty and the other for relatively "new" used cars. The old-used-car business is predominantly a private-party business today and is likely to become more so. Price sensitivity for buyer and seller is so high that there is little room for a middleman. But it is difficult to envision people ever selecting old cars remotely, because the information critical for making a purchasing decision *cannot be standardized*. Every old car, alas, is unique. Buyers need to see it, look for rust, try it out. The kind of information that can be communicated electronically will not suffice. However, navigators like Auto Trader and

CarPoint provide electronic classified advertising services to enable sellers and buyers to find each other. And they provide useful background data that facilitates searching and reduces information asymmetries: customer satisfaction data, model specifications, and wholesale and retail Blue Book prices.

The business of selling relatively new used cars—those that are one to three years old and whose quality is therefore high—is a different story. Quality standards can enable the buyers of newer cars to narrow their selection remotely, and there is enough margin to allow room for intermediaries. CarMax, for example, certifies its cars against a 115-point checklist and provides a guarantee of performance.[6] This does not mean that people will make a purchase without actually test-driving the car, but it does imply that on-line searching can narrow the range of choices more efficiently than for the old used cars, because of the possibility of standards. Standards create a role for a navigator, either CarMax actually buying, certifying, and selling the car, or some organization like AAA certifying the quality for a fee and thus supporting direct sale between private parties.

One physical function remains: the test drive. This would appear to be the only one where the dealer is competitively advantaged. However, even the test drive, one could argue, could be better provided by Hertz.

We describe the deconstruction of the auto dealer hypothetically, although most of this is already happening. Players such as Autobytel, Auto Trader, Carfax, CarMax, CarPoint, J.D. Power, Midas Muffler, financial institutions, and even (some of) the manufacturers are chipping away at an edifice that is on the verge of collapse. Competitively disadvantaged in every component in their service bundle and faced with the melting of whatever glue held that bundle together, the dealers are doomed to deconstruction, somehow, at some point. But there are countervailing forces holding the structure together. The car manufacturers have an enormous investment in their current dealer networks; indeed, the dealer network is a major component in their (currently defined) competitive advantage. It would be easier for them (paradoxically) to blow up the whole structure if they owned it and could take strategic control. But they are tied by the franchise laws, which are administered in the United States by the states. And dealers seem to wield inordinate influence in state politics.

These factors may hold things up, twist the course of deconstruction into irrational contortions, and cause the collapse, when it does come, to be more precipitous than would otherwise be the case. But they will not prevent it. The smarter manufacturers are already—cautiously, discreetly—beginning to move.

Implications of Deconstruction for Competitive Advantage

By transforming business and industry structure, deconstruction alters the sources of competitive advantage. The shifts will occur at different speeds and with varying intensities from industry to industry, but the consequences are the same for all businesses or industries vulnerable to deconstruction.

Competitive Advantage Is "De-Averaged"

As value chains deconstruct, they will fragment into multiple businesses that have separate sources of competitive advantage. This results in the de-averaging of competitive advantage. When all the functions in a value chain are bundled together, what matters is competitive advantage *over the entire chain*. As long as the sum is advantaged, it does not matter where specifically that advantage comes from, still less whether the business is advantaged in each constituent activity. Car dealers have managed to survive despite being disadvantaged in almost every aspect of their chain, when each is viewed in isolation. Superiority in some functions offsets mediocrity in others.

But when a value chain is deconstructed, this logic unravels. Advantage on average no longer matters. Companies can no longer subsidize poor performance in one activity by combining it with others in which they are advantaged. In each separable activity, new competitors emerge who focus on maximizing performance in just that specific step. Banks are attacked by financial specialists, car dealers by local repair shops. So to survive, a competitor has to be advantaged in each and every activity in which he chooses to continue participation.

Competition Escalates

Integrated value chains are subject to a "law of large numbers." When multiple and independent sources of competitive advantage are bundled and added together, differences in their total are proportionately less than differences in the components of that sum. Advantages in some activities offset disadvantages in others, so competitive advantage in the aggregate tends to "net out." The aggregation implicit in the integrated value chain thus *attenuates* overall competitive advantage, which is why in most businesses so many competitors are able to survive and prosper.

But within each new, narrowly defined business, fewer bases of competitive advantage prevail (by definition). With fewer ways to win, there is less "netting out" of competitive advantage. With fewer ways to win, there are fewer winners. Where there is only one basis of competitive advantage, monolithic advantage tends to breed monopoly. Where there is none at all, lack of advantage breeds stalemate. In all of the post-deconstruction businesses, their comparative simplicity intensifies competition.

Information Businesses Inherit New Value

Deconstruction leads to the segregation of informational from physical businesses, as with car dealers. It is easy to think of these information businesses as attractive perhaps, but minor and peripheral. This can be very wrong. IBM thought at one point that the operating system was a minor informational adjunct to the PC business.

If information is the locus of competitive advantage, then the information business will be where the competitive advantage, and therefore the profits, and therefore the shareholder value, are retained. The fact that such businesses may be smaller and less established than their physical siblings is quite beside the point.

This makes the question of whether or not to participate in such businesses much more acute. For a newspaper publisher, bank, or car manufacturer, these information businesses are profoundly different enterprises: businesses that operate on a set of economics, motivations, management style, clock speed, and risk appetite totally alien to the corporations' long-established, procedural ways of doing business. Yet success, even survival, may depend on learning to play that game.

Information Businesses Follow Different, and More Intense, Rules of Competitive Advantage

Competitive advantage in physical businesses derives from a broadly understood set of principles: economies of scale, segmentation, operational effectiveness, and the like. Information businesses are quite different. Setting and controlling standards, achieving preemptive critical mass, controlling patents and copyrights, making alliances, adapting to an order-of-magnitude shift in the underlying technology every five years, shifting the business boundaries—these are the drivers of competitive advantage. And the degree of competitive advantage that can be achieved is much greater. As we argued in chapter 2, there is a fundamental logic why information businesses are either monopolies or they are not businesses at all. Competitive dynamics are therefore a race for that monopoly position, and the winner often takes all.

New Opportunities Arise for Physical Businesses

In many businesses today, the efficiency of the physical value chain is compromised for the purposes of delivering information. The new economics of information therefore creates opportunities to rationalize the logistical value chain and build businesses whose physically based sources of competitive advantage are more sustainable.

Federal Express and UPS are among the biggest potential winners from the growth of electronic commerce. Supermarkets can take over the cash dispensing and collection function from banks. Hertz can provide the test drive. In dozens of businesses, the focused provider of physical services, uncompromised by informational distractions (except insofar as they relate to logistics), is a big future winner.

In some cases, the physical business proves a surprising source of competitive advantage. Consider the celebrated example of electronic book selling. Amazon.com, an electronic retailer on the Web, has no physical stores and started with very little inventory. It offers an electronic list of three million books, twenty times larger than that of the largest chain store.[7] Customers can search through that catalog via the Web. Amazon, in its early days, ordered almost all of its books from two industry wholesalers in response to customers' requests. It then unpacked, repacked, and mailed them from its distribution facility in Seattle.

Amazon established a variety of informational advantages: the three-million-item catalog, a user-friendly interface, reviews, customized recommendations, and so forth. But there is nothing obviously defensible about all this. The database is owned and operated by the wholesalers (originally for the benefit of small bookshops) and is open to anybody. The interface, reviews, and recommendations are easy to replicate. And by double-handling the books, Amazon incurred unnecessary physical costs.

Had Amazon sat still, the wholesalers could have put dozens of Amazons into business. Indeed, they could have created a lower-cost distribution system by encouraging portals like Yahoo! to serve as pure navigators, paying them a finder's fee, and then selling and shipping the book directly to the consumer. That would have eliminated the double handling. Electronic retailers would then have become mere search engines connected to somebody else's database, adding little value and achieving little competitive advantage. The wholesalers would be the big winners.

However, the electronic booksellers did *not* sit still. Amazon is growing its inventory, building regional distribution centers, and backward integrating into wholesaling. And Barnes & Noble tried to acquire the largest wholesaler, Ingram, whose platform originally put Amazon into business. In the battle of the books, it is physical logistics as much as informational franchise that will determine the winner.

Many Wholesalers, Retailers, and Distributors Will Be Disintermediated

When providers and users of information can deal with each other directly, and when physical flows can be rationalized in parallel, intermediaries often become obsolete. Working in tandem, facilitators of a new information flow and of a new physical flow can end-run the established intermediary. Microsoft navigates, and Ford delivers. Amazon navigates, and Ingram and UPS deliver. Disintermediation, as we will argue in chapter 5, threatens to undermine a wide range of established businesses with a scope and intensity that are unprecedented.

Deconstruction and Strategy "Frameworks"

In his classic work *Competitive Strategy,* Professor Michael Porter identified "five forces" that drive industry competition: rivalry among existing firms, the threat of new entrants, threats from substitute products or services, the bargaining power of suppliers, and the bargaining power of buyers.*

The logic of deconstruction contradicts none of this. But it does throw into question all the entities that Professor Porter's framework takes as self-evident. In a deconstructing world, the competitors, substitutes, suppliers, and customers—indeed, the identity and boundaries of the "business" and "industry" that the framework purports to analyze—must themselves become the focus of careful thought. The five forces cannot be applied without first determining what precisely are the objects on which those forces act. Deconstruction redefines those objects.

In their classic article "The Core Competence of the Corporation," Professors Gary Hamel and C. K. Prahalad suggested that "competencies" owned and nurtured by the corporation are its critical resource and competitive asset, and that the corporation should therefore consist of a portfolio of businesses that variously contribute to, or extract value from, those core competencies.** Implicit in this idea is the assumption that competencies can flow richly *within* the corporate boundary but not so richly *across* them: a richness/reach trade-off.

The logic of deconstruction contradicts none of this. However, it does suggest that the model of core competencies may be a special case. Competencies may belong to an individual, a team, a business, a corporation, or a regional economy (such as Silicon Valley or Wall Street). Competencies are a basis of corporate identity and strategy only when the semantically rich community that nurtures them happens to coincide with the boundaries of the corporation. That may, or may not, be the case. Shifts in the richness/reach trade-off change the answer.

---

*Michael E. Porter, *Competitive Strategy: Techniques for Analyzing Industries and Competitors,* (New York: The Free Press, 1980).

**Gary Hamel and C. K. Prahalad, "The Core Competence of the Corporation," *Harvard Business Review,* May–June 1990.

Navigators Emerge

Deconstruction implies choice. Choice, beyond a certain point, implies bewilderment. Hence the rise of the navigator. Navigators may be software programs (such as Quicken), databases (Auto Trader), evaluators (*Consumer Reports,* J.D.

Power), or search engines (Yahoo!). They can also be people: in a deconstructed financial universe, many affluent families will rely on financial advisers to help them make complex choices. Many readers will still want their daily news filtered and prioritized by a human editorial team that they respect and trust. Navigation may look like a small business, but it is likely to be the fulcrum around which competitive advantage hinges. The rise of navigators as independent businesses is destined to be one of the most dramatic aspects of deconstruction. It is also destined (as we will argue in chapters 6, 7, and 8) to drive fundamental power shifts among the other players.

The Challenge to the Incumbent

Incumbents can behave like the owners of *Britannica*. They can become paralyzed by their reluctance to cannibalize their established business model. Newspapers pricing themselves out of the business in an attempt to maintain revenues; banks ganging up to create a standard that limits the customer's ability to make choice; car manufacturers trying to mollify their dealers by refusing to deal with new distribution channels: all are pursuing strategies eerily similar to those that led *Britannica* to its downfall.

The paralysis of the leading incumbent is the greatest competitive advantage enjoyed by new competitors. It is an advantage that they often do not deserve, since if the incumbent would only fight all-out by the new rules, the incumbent would often win. The paralysis of the leading incumbent is also the greatest competitive advantage for the *marginal* incumbent, who has lost the old game and has every motive to change the rules. Deconstructed distribution, for example, is a huge opportunity for *offshore* car manufacturers, since they have inferior conventional distributor networks and more to gain than lose from blowing them up.

It is difficult to downsize assets that have high fixed costs when so many customers still prefer the current business model. It is difficult to cannibalize current profits. It is difficult to walk away from core competencies that were built over decades, the object of personal and collective pride and identity. And it can be even harder to squeeze the profits of partners and distributors to whom one is tied by long-standing relationships or contractual obligation.

But a greater vulnerability than legacy assets is a legacy mindset. It may be easy to grasp this point intellectually, but it is profoundly difficult in practice. Managers must put aside the presuppositions of the old competitive world and compete according to totally new rules of engagement. They must make decisions at a different speed, long before the numbers are in place and the plans formalized. They must acquire totally new technical and entrepreneurial skills, quite different from what made their organization (and them personally) so successful. They must manage for maximal opportunity, not minimum risk. They must devolve decision making, install different reward structures, and perhaps even devise different ownership structures. They have little choice. If they don't deconstruct their own businesses, somebody else will do it to them.

SOUND BITS

- A little deconstruction does a lot of damage; deconstruction will strike where the incumbent can least afford it.

- The insurgent's greatest competitive advantage is the unwillingness of the incumbent to fight on a deconstructed definition of the business.

- Deconstruction is followed by reconstruction. New business definitions emerge from the ruins of the old.

- Navigators are a new function, a new industry, a new competitive opportunity. In many businesses (as defined today) the navigator will appropriate most of the value.

- When a value chain begins to deconstruct, almost any choice of focus is better than clinging to an obsolete, integrated business definition.

5

DISINtERMEDIATION

$\mathbf{m}$ANY, IF NOT MOST, intermediaries make their living from the trade-off between richness and reach. Blow it up, and these intermediaries get blown up as well. At the very least, when the original supplier of goods or services and the ultimate consumer can deal directly with each other, the intermediary has to make a new case for his continued existence. The destruction of the old intermediary function—disintermediation—is the focus of this chapter. The development of the new intermediary function—navigation—is the focus of the next.

Two factors make intermediaries vulnerable: an embedded compromise between the economics of things and the economics of information, and a compromise between richness and reach. Either is sufficient, but if neither applies, no cumulation of technical breakthroughs will have the slightest impact on the structure of the business.

Two Forms of Disintermediation

Disintermediation is not new. Bankers used the term in the 1970s to describe how securities markets displaced corporate banking and how money market funds captured a large portion of deposits from retail banks.[1] What is new, however, is the nature of the disintermediation that is driven by the new economics of information, and its speed and impact on existing intermediaries.

There are two basic forms of disintermediation: moving along the current richness/reach curve toward greater reach, and displacing the curve itself. The first is old. The second is new (see Figure 5-1).

In the traditional story of disintermediation, the new competitor attacks the established intermediary by offering greater reach and less richness. He focuses on customers

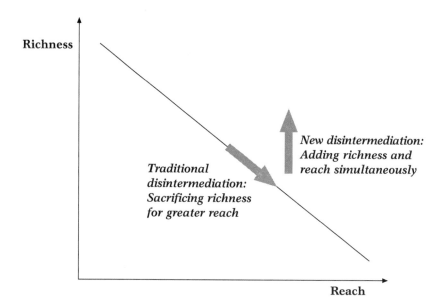

Figure 5-1: The Two Forms of Disintermediation

who are hard to reach or customers who place less value on the richness provided by the traditional intermediary. He typically offers a lower-cost version of the product or service. This is a *different* value proposition and not necessarily a superior one. It does not destroy the established intermediary, but it does re-segment the market. Frequently, in fact, disintermediators expand the market by addressing the needs of some previously ignored but significant group of customers.

When the Sears and Roebuck Company introduced its catalog in the late nineteenth century, it disintermediated hundreds of local hardware and clothing stores.[2] The catalog offered a significantly less rich interface than the country store: two-dimensional rather than three-dimensional product displays and brief paragraphs of text rather than interactive cracker-barrel wisdom from the sales clerk. But it offered greater *reach*: a much wider selection of products and the ability to deliver to remote locations. Sears separated the physical and the informational functions traditionally bundled together in the country store. It employed a cheaper, less-labor-intensive means of delivering information and a cheaper, more-scale-intensive means of fulfilling orders. It substituted reach for richness.

Sears offered a *different* trade-off between richness and reach, not necessarily a superior one. For some purposes, both physical and informational, the country store continued to be advantaged. In consequence, both disintermediated and intermediated business solutions coexisted. Indeed, Sears catalogs coexisted with Sears's own stores.

Other disintermediations have followed the same pattern. Term life insurance has substituted for a substantial portion of the traditional whole life business: term is largely sold directly to consumers, employing high-reach/low-richness methods, while whole life products continue to be distributed mainly through agents, a high-richness/low-reach channel. ATMs have substituted in part for bank tellers. Voice mail has substituted in part for secretaries.

The second and more radical form of disintermediation occurs when technology allows for the richness/reach curve to be displaced, allowing new players to offer greater reach and greater richness simultaneously. This poses a far more direct threat to the established intermediary's business model. It threatens not just a re-segmentation of the business, but a transformation.

Disintermediations driven by players exploiting the new economics of information have a way of starting very conventionally: the substitution of reach for richness. It is only late in the story that the sting in the tail becomes apparent: the possibility of a new richness that overwhelms the traditional intermediaries. And the traditional intermediaries, thinking that all they face is a re-segmentation (and invariably convinced that their high-richness segment is the place to be), then discover too late how fundamental is the threat to their business model.[3] Stock brokerage is a case in point.

The Brokerage Business

Stock brokerage is a pure information business. The brokerage house offers access to financial markets and the ability to execute trades. The individual broker serves as an intermediary between the client and the executional capabilities of his employer. In addition to taking trading instructions from the client, the broker provides financial advice and brings new investment opportunities to the client's attention.

Until 1975, brokerage commissions were regulated. Since houses could not compete on price, they competed on personal service and the perceived quality of their investment advice. The individual broker was paid on commission and therefore had an incentive to generate as much trading volume as possible, whether that was in the client's interests or not. But the best brokers developed rich personal relationships with their clients: lunches, phone calls, and personal friendships were all part of the job. Reach was constrained by the number of relationships that a broker could sustain.

The relationships nurtured by good brokers were so close, in fact, that when they switched from one house to another, they were able to take a large portion of their client list with them. For the brokerage houses, this drained a lot of the value out of the business: unless they paid a big producer something close to the full economic value of the book of business he owned, they risked losing the broker *and* the business to a competitor who was not so inhibited. Brokerage houses found themselves competing for brokers, to the point where the broker—the intermediary—was effectively the customer. Sales force "churn" became the biggest managerial challenge.

In the early 1980s Merrill Lynch, closely followed by other brokerage houses, introduced the Cash Management Account, a revolutionary application of information technology. The CMA enabled clients to integrate different kinds of asset and credit accounts, sweep funds automatically across those accounts, and manage their affairs from a single integrated statement. It created a powerful incentive for clients to place all their assets with the brokerage house. It also created substantial switching costs for the client who wanted to move to another brokerage house. It thus locked in the relationship between client and brokerage house and weakened the leverage of the intermediating broker. Technology had been used to create an informational glue to bind client, broker, and brokerage house into a stable franchise, controlled by the latter. Churn became manageable.

In 1975, when the Securities and Exchange Commission ended the regime of fixed commissions and deregulated the business, most firms *raised* their commissions.[4] But Charles Schwab decided to position his small company quite differently. He created the first discount brokerage, a high-reach/low-richness player. The firm provided no personalized advice but executed transactions for about half the prices charged by Merrill Lynch.[5] Schwab focused on self-directed clients who were frequent traders, investors who didn't need or believe the advice provided by the full-service firms and found their prices excessive. Schwab offered this segment a simple transactional capability, executed over the phone through an anonymous operator. Revenues grew from $4.6 million in 1977 to $126 million in 1983.[6]

As the company grew, it was able to achieve scale economies in its back office operations. Schwab operated from a few national service centers staffed by low-cost order takers. The full-service competitors could not do the same without compromising staff quality or geographic proximity, both of which were central to their high-richness strategy.

In 1989, Schwab introduced a Touch-Tone service, which allowed customers to conduct transactions at any time of the day or night without talking to a customer representative: another extension of reach. In 1995, Schwab handled sixty million calls, or 75 percent of its total call volume, in this manner, accounting for about eleven million trades.[7]

Contrary to many early prognoses, the rise of the discount brokerage houses did not destroy the full-service business. Despite the discount segment's high growth, its share of New York Stock Exchange commissions had increased to only 15 percent in 1997, and much of that volume was probably new business encouraged by the low transactions fees. Full-service firms were secure in the high-richness/low-reach segment of the market, where personal relationships, investment advice, and reassurance matter more than cheap and remote execution.

On-line Trading

The proliferation in the early 1990s of personal computers with modems allowed for a much richer interface than the twelve keys of the telephone. The pioneer was E*Trade, which began on-line operations in 1992 and was able to undercut the discount brokers because it did not have to support the cost of call centers. Schwab recognized that it would have to create an all-electronic, deep-discount version of its brokerage offering to remain competitive, so in 1996 it introduced e.Schwab. Initially, only customers who opened separate e.Schwab accounts could trade electronically, but transactions were priced at $39 per trade, a 50 percent discount from standard fees at the time. The company risked cannibalizing an enormous part of its business, and more than 50 percent of the 700,000 on-line accounts that Schwab had opened by May 1997 came from its 4.2 million regular accounts.[8]

As the Internet took off, the number of electronic brokers rose to over seventy. Competition intensified. The deepest of deep discounters drove the price below $10 per trade. In January 1998, Schwab lowered its standard transaction price for Internet trades to $29.95 per trade and made on-line trading available to all customers, not just those who opened e.Schwab accounts.

In parallel, Schwab fought back against the deep discounters by offering greater richness. All customers were given access to Schwab's high-quality information services offerings: brand-name research reports, portfolio tracking, records management, and the full panoply of CMA-type cash

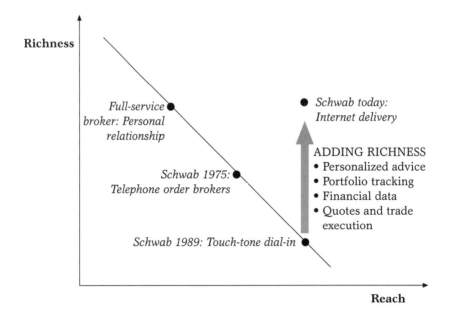

Figure 5-2: On-line Brokers: Blowing Up the Richness/Reach Trade-off

management services such as money market and checking accounts (see Figure 5-2).

But a universe of investment information and advice was becoming available on the Web anyway. Whether using e.Schwab or Quicken, or simply by surfing with Netscape, investors can find, filter, and customize an array of investment information. Yahoo! and Pointcast can track a portfolio and provide alerts on specific companies of interest. The Motley Fool is well known for detailed stock analyses. At BestCalls.com, investors can listen in on company earnings announcements with analysts. Intuit has added features like College Planner to its Quicken financial management program to help users make long-term financial decisions. Standard & Poor's offers a site that makes stock and mutual fund recommendations based on an individual's financial objectives and assets. The mutual fund databases of Lipper and Morning-star are available on-line. Small companies like financial-engines.com offer sophisticated portfolio optimization, using algorithms originally developed for institutional investors.

Today, an investor who trades electronically over the Internet or over a private network can access world-class investment analysis and news, and get tailored analyses and real-time price quotes. The next generation of OFX, the financial information standard, will provide a universal way to order and confirm stock market transactions, enabling investors to keep accounts with multiple institutions and integrate their statements by using financial management software. The quality of the information and advice available on-line is better than that available from any one stock-broker. And it is not compromised by any conflict of interest.

Small wonder, then, that on-line trading has experienced such phenomenal growth. Piper Jaffray estimated that this channel accounted for 37 percent of retail stock and option trades in 1998.[9]

The Competitive Struggle

On-line brokers, operating in seamless consort with Internet information providers, can raise the richness of their services without apparent limit. They can offer the user reach to an unlimited universe of sources and services. And the full-service brokers have hardly moved: their offerings, their pricing, and even, if truth be told, the sophistication of their services are little different today from what they were ten or fifteen years ago. The trade-off between their richness and the discounter's reach, which had defined competitive segmentation since 1975, has become totally obsolete. They are beaten in both dimensions.

But there is one aspect of richness—one critical aspect—that technology cannot match: the human interface. Many investors simply don't want to deal with databases and analytics. They don't want to "take control" of their affairs and spend Saturday mornings staring at spreadsheets. They want advice from a broker, *their* broker, who has hot information and is undivided in his loyalties. Above all, they crave emotional support when the market turns down; they need human reassurance when long-term investment strategies face short-term reversals. No "intelligent agent" can do that. These people may constitute a small segment, a shrinking segment, possibly an aging segment. But it is also a very affluent segment, and one that cares little for price. Even if it is only 10 percent of the market, it is worth more at $100 per trade than the rest of the market at $10 per trade.

But herein lies the catch. Schwab discovered in the early nineties that half of its customers for an integrated product, called the Schwab One Account, maintained multiple accounts and had their statements mailed to multiple addresses. It turned out that these customers were actually independent financial advisers, who were using the Schwab platform for transactions and statements, but offering their clients precisely the kind of personal, human services that Merrill Lynch offered, and Schwab did not. Schwab was *not* in fact at a disadvantage in serving the personal service segment: it was already doing so in league with an army of former Merrill Lynch brokers.

All the capabilities targeted by Schwab and everybody else at the "take charge" investor have become equally and equivalently available to the passive investor's personal financial adviser. Since Schwab and its fellow discounters have ten times the volume, they are far lower cost and will quickly build better scale-sensitive transaction technology. Since they have ten times the reach, they have a better array of information, advice, and analytics. As a platform for the advisory business they are better quality, more comprehensive, and cheaper. The passive investor may not know or care, but the financial adviser is *in the business* of knowing.

Which brings the logic full circle. Only the best brokers will be tempted to leave the cozy environment of a full-service house and go independent. They will be tempted because they know how much money the brokerage house pockets off their efforts. To keep them, the brokerage house will have to give them back the value that they generate. So the residual value of personal relationships, the one part of the business that technology cannot deconstruct, will indeed survive, and will flourish, but it will flourish as a cottage industry outside the control of the brokerage houses, or within the houses but on the brokers' terms. The logic of deconstruction may fail to break the relationship between some clients and their advisers because there are kinds of richness that technology cannot deliver. But in consequence of that very fact it will break the bond between the adviser and his erstwhile employer.

Winners and Losers

The business model of the full-service brokerage house can work profitably only if it can persuade enough customers, as well as its brokers, that its collective capabilities, multiple experts, special access to unique investment opportunities, or its umbrella brand translate into superior quality or value. That may not be easy. CEO rhetoric notwithstanding, the culture of a full-service brokerage is based on transactions, not advice. The revenue structure is based on transactions. The real advice needs of all but the richest clients are not that high. The quality of the advice actually given is not systematically advantaged and not always objective. Access to "unique" investment opportunities (or at least uniquely good ones) is largely a myth. And converting a brokerage house into an association of professional investment counselors who share a common brand is not easy. The more successful a broker is, the less valuable the brand is to him, and the more the house has to pay to keep him—and his clients—in the fold.

The deep-discount electronic brokers may look like the obvious winners. They threaten to disintermediate everyone else by merit of their single-minded focus on the low-cost/high-reach channel. They can add richness, or simply allow their customers to get richness independently through the seamless connectivity of the Internet. Moore's Law is on their side. Processing glitches will be ironed out. Customers will steadily become more sophisticated, more confident, and therefore more willing to unbundle and buy on price. The problem for the deep discounters is that they are trapped in a purely "commodity" definition of the business. In an environment of excess capacity, price wars that lead to marginal-cost pricing could drive margins permanently negative. In the euphoric phase for Internet stocks, this may not seem to matter too much, but at some point expectations have to be realized, and that, for the deep discounters, could be a challenge.

Schwab is fighting a war on two fronts: against the full-service brokerages and the price-based electronic traders. Against the full-service brokerages, it can continue to play aggressive disintermediator, newly strengthened by the richness that the firm can add to its traditional advantages in reach. But against E*Trade, Schwab has to compete on quality, service, and trust for the favors of customers who have already declared themselves to be price-sensitive. Even in a world of seamless connectivity, an integrated and branded bundle has value for some clients, and Schwab is investing heavily to market just that. Some premium is almost certainly sustainable, especially supporting independent financial advisers and investors with more complex needs. But just how high that premium is, and just what bundle of richness will be required to sustain it, remain open questions. There is no simple endgame. In many ways, the clearest strategy prescription is the one that Schwab has followed so consistently: the willingness to be ruthless in disintermediating oneself.

Personal Computer Retailing

Despite the high-tech product, selling personal computers is a physical business. In this business, disintermediation began, as with the Sears catalog, by breaking the mutual compromise between the economics of things and the economics of information—an issue that never arose in stock brokerage. But as with stock brokerage, what started as a conventional substitution of reach for richness has evolved into a blowup of the trade-off between them.

In the early years of the personal computer industry, most customers were first-time buyers, hardware and software specifications were difficult to understand, and "plug-and-play" was a pipe dream. If the thing went wrong, troubleshooting was a nightmare. This made buying a PC complex, risky, and nerve-wracking. Customers needed to try out the machine before purchase and they needed after-sales support from someone who understood the technologies, or at least the manuals. Independent (or franchised) computer stores, manned by a trained, often evangelical sales staff, evolved to meet these needs.

This distribution system was extremely successful. By 1987, computer retailing in the United States had grown to a $5.8 billion business.[10] At the time, dealers and direct sales forces, which provided detailed explanations of their products, accounted for two-thirds of industry sales. However, in the following ten years, these intermediaries who provided customer hand-holding generated only 26 percent of the units sold.[11]

The first attack on the small computer dealership came from mass marketers. Specialist retailers, such as CompUSA, entered the market, along with established discount retailers, such as Best Buy and Office Depot. They followed their usual "big-box" strategy of massive selection and low prices, which they achieved through in-store operating economies, quick inventory turns, and efficient warehouse distribution. They did not offer the same level of technical sales expertise that the small dealers did, because consumers were becoming more sophisticated and the product was getting more modular. Consumers cared less about hand-holding and more about price and selection. In a fashion that retailing has seen dozens of times, the category killers substituted reach for richness.

Dell Computer Corporation, incorporated in 1984, carried this substitution of reach for richness much further by selling personal computers directly to consumers. The company had no dealer network at all, relying solely on a mail-order catalog and order taking by telephone and fax.

The economics of direct sales proved spectacular. One of the basic problems in the computer industry is that the costs of holding inventory are extraordinarily high: not through slow turns, but because of rapid obsolescence. Retail prices of some mid- to high-end PCs drop an average of 7 percent per month.[12] By selling from a catalog, Dell was able to offer selection without tying it to in-store inventory, separating the bond between inventory and product selection. This presumed, correctly, that consumers were willing to sacrifice the richness of in-store trial. But by making that sacrifice, the company was then able to rationalize its newly liberated economics of things by manufacturing largely to order. This eliminated most of the finished goods inventory that is such an expensively wasting asset. As Michael Dell put it, "We substitute information for inventory and ship only when we have demand from real end consumers."[13]

As of October 1998, Dell maintained only about eight days of inventory of components and finished products. Compaq, more typically, had about thirty-five days of inventory, and its resellers carried another twenty-five days.[14] One research firm estimates that this translates into cost of goods sold being 6 percent lower for Dell, an enormous advantage in a low-margin, price-sensitive business.[15] On the basis of this disintermediating strategy, Dell's annual sales have rocketed to $16.7 billion and the company continues to grow at over 50 percent per year.[16]

On-line PC Retailing: Adding Richness

More recently, Dell has started selling over the Internet. As with Schwab, this has allowed the company to move off the richness/reach trade-off. Through Dell's Web site, customers can access detailed product line descriptions and can use "configurator" software that allows them to select among a wide range of options. Customers can design the exact configuration they want and see instantaneously the price implications of the choices they make. An obvious next step will be for Dell's interface to start from *needs* and then guide the customer to configurations appropriate to the applications being run. Conjoint technology could determine the weight customers implicitly attach to alternative features (including

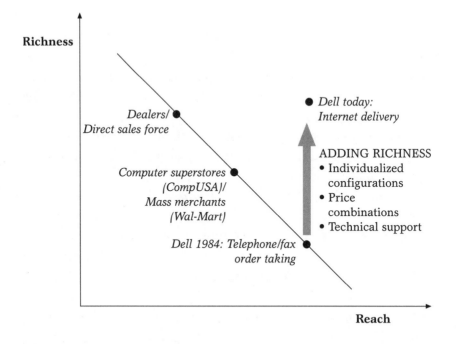

**Figure 5-3: Computer Retailing: Blowing Up the Richness/
Reach Trade-off**

price) and then choose the closest approximation within the
Dell product line (see Figure 5-3).

Dell has also increased richness by offering corporate
buyers product information directly on their own intranets.
The information is customized for each account, restricting
choice to preapproved configurations and offering them at
company-negotiated discounts.

The company is further extending richness by providing
on-line technical support. Like most computer companies,
Dell had developed elaborate and sophisticated decision-
support software to help its own technical staff troubleshoot
problems. When a customer calls Dell with a technical prob-

lem, the support engineer uses the software to identify and solve that problem. Some business customers are now able to access the entire Dell troubleshooting system directly. By allowing them to tap directly into the database, Dell offers twenty-four-hour reach and up-to-the-minute richness, and saves money by disintermediating its own service representatives. Also, by allowing customers to go down their own learning curve with the troubleshooting system, Dell builds in a significant cost for them to switch to the support systems of any competitor.

Dell also has extended this richness back into its supply chain. In what Michael Dell terms "virtual integration," the company coordinates the supply chain by exchanging information with suppliers electronically. Essentially, Dell brings suppliers into its business much more than traditional OEMs by sharing production scheduling, demand forecasts, and other information in a timely manner via the Internet. The entire supply chain becomes linked by information, allowing Dell to reduce response time, eliminate even more inventory, and meet changing customer needs very quickly.[17]

Competitors have been skewered by Dell's strategy, not because it is hard to understand, but because it is politically difficult to replicate when their current customer base is an established dealer network. One response, by IBM and others, is to move some final assembly into the dealerships, eliminating inventory through assemble-to-order, but preserving something for the dealer to do. Whether dealers can ever be as efficient in assembly as factories remains an open question, but it does ameliorate part of the cost penalty.

Much as Toyota did in its development of kanban (just-in-time) manufacture, Dell has implemented a fundamentally new economics of things. It centers on the radical substitution of "pull" for "push" as the paradigm of production.

Instead of forecasting demand, Dell simply responds to it. Instead of directing suppliers, Dell allows them to look directly into its network and respond to the signals they see. Instead of using inventory as a buffer against uncertainty, Dell has eliminated most of the production lags that made inventory necessary.

In parallel, Dell has implemented a fundamentally new economics of information. Its on-line presence is evolving into a continuous source of support and problem solving. If Dell can continue to grow that presence, it will evolve into a navigator far richer, and reaching far further into consumers' daily usage of their computer systems. Such a supportive relationship, as it grows, will be far more intimate and informed, far more compelling than any sales pitch, even a human one.

The physical strategy and the informational strategy become so powerful, and so sustainable, once each is released from the burden of having to support the other.

The Limits of Disintermediation

In brokerage, disintermediators displaced the trade-off between richness and reach; in PC retailing their primary impact was splitting the economics of things and the economics of information. Both succeeded because embedded in the prior business model was a *compromise*: between richness and reach, between information and things. Often, however, the logic looks the same, but the compromise is simply not severe enough, at least in relation to current ability to displace it. Here the would-be disintermediators are destined to be disappointed. Consider the grocery and catalog retailing businesses.

The On-line Grocery Business

Three companies (among others) in the United States are currently pioneering on-line grocery shopping: Peapod, Streamline, and NetGrocer. All three offer the informational benefits of ordering groceries on-line. Standard items can be entered by default. Unusual items are easy to search for. Budgeting is transparent. The user can be prompted with the family's regular brand preferences. Sellers can present special offers and customized discounts. Nutritional and recipe information can be cross-referenced. In the not-too-distant future, a smart refrigerator could do some of the ordering unprompted.

But it is not clear that the difference in *informational* functionality between a notepad and a computer screen is really the reason why many would choose to use one of these services. The reason, if any, is *physical*: avoiding the trip to the store, the queuing, and the stress involved in shopping in a supermarket—to say nothing of the time it all takes. And the real question is how big a premium, if any, the home-maker will be willing to pay to avoid the burden of physical shopping.

Peapod, which serves over a hundred thousand customers in seven metropolitan areas, purchases products directly from wholesalers and specialty providers.[18] This results in higher costs for consumers as Peapod cannot get the volume discounts of large chains, and delivery costs are tacked on to each order. Apart from the nutritional cross-references or the capacity to connect to the smart refrigerator, there is little value outside of delivery convenience. For a segment of busy and affluent families, the service is clearly worth the premium, but if there were real pent-up demand, it would probably have been realized years before the Internet.

From Your Perspective

If You Are a Retailer . . .

- Don't assume that your current franchise is worth that much. Already, in many retailing categories, consumers are changing behavior quickly.

- Look at how you compromise the economics of information and the economics of things. Is your "warehouse" really efficient when viewed as a pure distribution system? Does your "billboard" (or product offering and display) really offer the alternatives that consumers want and need?

If You Are a Supplier . . .

- Here's your chance to wrest the consumer relationship away from your retailers. Go for it before an e-retailer does.

- It's easy to be lulled into thinking you are best positioned for the direct-to-consumer relationship; yet in most categories new players are leading the battle. Key to your success is understanding how to play in the new environment and how to use your capabilities to advantage.

- Beware of the e-retailer. He may become the next Wal-Mart.

- Beware of the impartial navigator. He succeeds to the extent that he commoditizes your business.

- Encourage efficient, objective search if you think you have a better mousetrap. Make sure your mousetrap is *sustainably* better. Most aren't.

- Be ready to confront conflicts—with your old organization structure, your old strategies, your strongest current sources of competitive advantage. Many of your old capabilities were built around managing the intermediary; now they need to be built around the consumer.

- Do not allow the objections of your current retailers to prevent you from doing the right thing by the consumer.

If You Are a New Player . . .

- Focus quickly on where the biggest compromises lie in the current business model; ensure that your first offering is directly targeted at these compromises.

- Recognize that deconstruction is a process—while the first wave of deconstruction may be about unlocking physical value, the second is often about informational value. Prepare for both moves. Continually deconstruct your own business model.

- Don't try to do it all; be ruthless in your use of outsourced business systems where they are not strategically essential.

- Keep your eye on new deconstructors entering from other consumer categories; in many cases, your most dangerous competitor is not the retailer or supplier in the current category but an adjacent player.

Streamline, which currently operates only in Boston, fills orders directly from its own 56,000-square-foot warehouse and delivers to a special compartmentalized container installed in the customer's garage. In addition to the usual groceries, Streamline delivers laundry, video rentals, and processed film. By bypassing the local grocery store in favor of a warehouse, Streamline substitutes cheap wholesale for expensive retail costs. But the total costs of the system depend critically on the volumes achieved. Higher volume means faster inventory turns, fewer stockouts, more efficient warehouse-style picking, more frequent deliveries, and above all, greater warehouse density and therefore shorter average transportation distances. At some sufficient volume, Streamline becomes as cheap as the grocery store. But that threshold volume is very high, far higher than the volumes achieved by any electronic grocery format.[19]

NetGrocer delivers from a single warehouse in New Jersey that carries only four thousand nonperishable items. Deliveries are made to the home via Federal Express.[20] The warehouse costs depend on national, not local, volume, which makes the scale threshold less intimidating, but unit delivery costs are obviously high and essentially independent of volume. For goods that are time-sensitive, perishable, fragile, heavy, or bulky, the physical economics of the system are prohibitive. NetGrocer could never substitute for all the family grocery shopping, just the portion that can be shipped economically from New Jersey.

Each of these three business models may find a niche, although it is interesting to note that Peapod recently announced plans for switching to the Streamline strategy by opening local warehouses in Chicago and Boston.[21] But none of them seems likely, in the foreseeable future, to transform the grocery business the way that Dell transformed computer retailing. Most grocery shoppers are price sensitive and place a low implicit value on their time. Fundamentally, physical grocery stores are pretty efficient already. Liberating the retailer's economics of things from the consumer's economics of information does not actually do much good. And within the economics of information, the richness/reach trade-offs embedded in the paper grocery list are not so severe. Special niches apart, grocery retailing is a target for disintermediation whose time has not yet come.

Catalog Retailing

Catalog retailing is often cited as a target for electronic disintermediation. People point to the obvious success of electronic retailers like Amazon.com and CDNOW, which are effectively in the electronic catalog business. But that misses the point. Amazon and CDNOW are *not* competing against catalog retailers, but against physical shops. Their success indicates nothing about the vulnerability of the paper catalog business, a vulnerability that is more apparent than real.

The catalog retailing business has *already* separated the economics of information from the economics of things: the former is the paper catalog, and the latter is the mail-order fulfillment operation. In many cases these are even owned and operated independently. As a result, when an electronic catalog substitutes for a paper one, the economics of physical distribution are unchanged. So (in contrast to Sears or Dell) there is *no* opportunity for a disintermediator to release economic value by separating the two economics: it has already been done. Any displacement of paper in the catalog business would have to be driven by the *informational* superiority of electronics.

A Web-based catalog has infinite depth; it is highly navigable; it can be continuously updated; it can accept and confirm orders on the spot; it can be customized with targeted offers; it costs almost nothing to distribute. There are problems with screen resolution, comparative color fidelity, and the slowness with which color photographs load. But these are transitional limitations; a few more iterations in the technology will change all that.

The problem with electronic versions of traditional paper catalogs is deeper. The paper catalog business is one of *casual perusal.* The whole point is not that people use catalogs in some purposeful way as they use the telephone directory (or, most of the time, Amazon.com), but rather that consumers find the catalog in their mail, leave it lying around the home, skim it casually, and buy something that they quite possibly never knew they wanted. Catalog retailing is the art of *engaging* the consumer. It is not clear that any Web-enabled device that requires booting, pointing, and clicking can function in the same way.

For catalog sellers whose content is the object of systematic and purposeful search, this is no objection, and they have taken successfully to the electronic format in direct consequence. Grainger, the industrial distributor, has had great success with the electronic version of its catalog: 30 percent of its on-line sales are to new customers or incremental sales to existing customers, and half of its on-line sales occur after its physical stores are closed.[22]

But for the more typical catalog retailer, the new medium has only supplementary value. That will change when full-motion video becomes common, combining the best features of home shopping television and electronic catalogs: a new kind of selling-as-entertainment will then develop. But since that is precisely what catalog retailers do today, there is little reason to doubt their ability to manage the transition to a new medium. So even if, or when, full-motion interactivity renders the paper catalog obsolete, it is still a fair bet that the catalog retailers of today will lead the transition, and not become its victims.

Winners and Losers

Traditional intermediaries generally combine physical functions with informational ones. Very broadly speaking, the physical functions are why the intermediary really exists, but the informational functions are the primary source of competitive differentiation, and thus profitability. Goods (of whatever form) must flow through the intermediary; the flow of goods provides advantaged access to the flow of information; and the intermediary is, therefore, able to collect tolls on that information flow.

Any separation of the economics of information from the economics of things upsets this basic equation. This has happened in the past, of course, but the enabling technology shifts have been slow and marginal. In these contexts, the newer disintermediating business model achieved lower cost and greater reach than the older model it attacked, but did so *only* by the sacrifice of some measure of richness. This carved out a segment of the market for the new model but left much of the traditional intermediated business untouched. The untouched segment often continued to be the highest-margin business. Provided that the disintermediation happened slowly enough and the overall market grew fast enough, the loss of market share by the traditional intermediary proved unpleasant but managerially tolerable.

However, when the underlying enabling technologies are moving an order of magnitude faster, the story is very different. The disintermediating business model can beat the old in both richness and reach. This can happen because technology permits more rich information to be delivered to consumers directly (e.g., Dell's configurator or Grainger's electronic catalog). It can also happen because technology permits such a thorough deconstruction of the old value chain that new combinations of free-standing players can match the capabilities of the old vertically integrated business model (e.g., independent brokers using the Schwab platform, providing the same personal service as the full-service broker).

Frequently Asked Questions

1. **Where will disintermediaton take place?**

   Wherever the richness/reach trade-off can be shifted *and* compromises in the current business are thereby eliminated. Both conditions are necessary. Disintermediation need not attack a whole "business" as conventionally defined. It can attack a part, even a small sliver, of a business. How the disintermediation unfolds depends on which player precipitates the attack.

2. **What defines the richness/reach trade-off that might be shifted?**

   Customer needs, not conventional business definitions.

3. **What sorts of compromises might be eliminated?**

   Either those arising from the linking of the economics of information to the economics of things, as Dell found in retail computer distribution, or those arising from the existence of the richness/reach trade-off itself, as Schwab discovered in stock brokerage. There may be any number of compromises embedded in current levels of richness that are only obvious to the consumer once the disintermediation proceeds.

4. **How is this disintermediation different from that of the past?**

   Previous disintermediations substituted reach for richness and therefore re-segmented the existing business. The new form of disintermediation adds radically more reach and then adds richness too. This does not re-segment the old business model. It destroys it.

5. **Which efforts at disintermediation are destined to fail?**

   Those that attack business models that do not contain significant compromises.

6. **Could my business be disintermediated?**

   Slivers of the business may be vulnerable. Those slivers often account for most, or all, of the value of the business.

7. **Where do I start?**

   Mentally deconstruct your business and look at the vulnerability of the pieces in terms of embedded compromises and potential for shifting richness/reach.

The vulnerability of the traditional intermediated business model depends critically on the extent to which the economics of information and the economics of things are mutually compromised and on the extent to which new combinations of richness and reach offer real value to the consumer. Computer stores proved vulnerable because of the mutual compromise. Full-service and traditional discount brokerages are vulnerable because of the new combinations of richness and reach. Conversely, groceries and consumer catalogs seem currently to be safe from major disintermediation because the embedded compromises between the physical and the informational are slight, and because the value of presenting information electronically, at least now, is simply not high enough.

When technologies are moving an order of magnitude faster, the incumbent no longer has the simple option of gracefully retreating to the high-margin segment. That was Britannica's mistake.

The losers in this new game of disintermediation will be players that may have been competitive in aggregate, but not in any one piece of a deconstructing value chain: for example, the unlamented auto dealer described in chapter 4. Any intermediating business could be vulnerable if it has what might be called "department store logic": one-stop shopping, cross-selling, cross-subsidies, all anchored on a putative "relationship" with the customer. And such businesses are especially vulnerable if the business system needs volume to cover high fixed costs, since a small loss of volume could mean a catastrophic decline in profits.

The winners in this new game of disintermediation will be the players who are good at *one thing,* or more precisely, the smaller number of things that define advantage in a deconstructed business definition. Delivery services such as Federal Express, efficient warehouse operators such as Wal-Mart, and even Schwab functioning as a brokerage transaction platform could gain massively from using their specialized, focused capabilities (physical or informational) to support the new intermediating models of others. Their volume potential depends on the pace of disintermediation; their profit potential depends on their ability to achieve physical economies of scale.

There will be winners on the informational side as well as the physical side. But they are not quite so simple to identify. Dell may be winning against computer stores and the computer companies that are locked into high-markup distribution channels that they dare not circumvent. But what if the customer bought her own configurator software? What if AOL got into the configuration business as a means of attracting traffic and advertising? Would Dell still be advantaged? It is to these questions—questions of competitive advantage in the purely informational "navigation" businesses—that we now turn.

SOUND BITS

- The only sure winner is the consumer.

- In a deconstructing world, "the business" is an artificial construct. Forget "the business." Focus on layers, specific information flows, specific physical functions. Each can be a separate battlefield.

- The only alternative to deconstructing your own consumer relationship is letting someone else deconstruct it for you.

- Disintermediation will occur in the layer, information flow, or physical function where the incumbent can least afford to let it happen.

- No assault on prevailing business structures will be left untried for lack of attention, capital, willingness to take risks, intelligence, or (for that matter) ignorance.

- The only sure loser is the "fast follower." Fast followers are *always* too late. It is better to be too early five times than to be too late once.

- The winner is *not* the player who understands the endgame. There is no endgame. The winner is the player who sees just one or two moves further ahead than the competitors.

- Assaults most frequently founder when they fail to liberate compromises embedded in the prevailing business model. Blowing up the richness/reach trade-off is necessary but not sufficient.

- Disintermediation used to be about substituting reach for richness. Now it is about transforming both, often simultaneously.

6

COMPETING ON REACH

ONE OF THE MOST IMPORTANT informational "glues" in the business world is the link to the consumer. Variously called "brand," "franchise," or "relationship," it is probably the most pervasive basis of competitive advantage in any consumer-focused business: far more important in general than cost position, product features, or technology. The strategy is to build in the consumer's mind a deep and locked-in relationship: richness that forecloses reach. Loyalty programs, advertising, data-based marketing, cross-selling, mass customization—almost all of the competitive initiatives that managers have focused on in recent years—target the consumer relationship. Competition to own the consumer is aggressive: retailer against retailer, supplier against supplier,[1] and also suppliers against their own retailers. Whoever owns the consumer relationship owns a partially noncompetitive annuity, whose lifetime value is often the value of the business.

Blowing up the richness/reach trade-off threatens to destroy that annuity, leaving *only* cost, product features, and technology as the remaining bases of competitive advantage. But it can also *shift* the annuity, allowing suppliers to reclaim the consumer relationship from retailers, or new players (such as electronic retailers or pure navigators) to steal it from incumbents. And it can also *redefine* the annuity, shifting it from one basis, such as search costs, to another, such as personal trust.

Once the richness/reach trade-off is blown up, suppliers, incumbent retailers, and new players compete against each other to own, or at least divide up, the consumer relationship: Mattel *versus* Toys R Us *versus* eToys; airlines *versus* travel agents *versus* Travelocity; Fidelity *versus* Citibank *versus* Intuit. They also *race* against each other: preemptive moves, alliances, strokes of transient luck, and tactical stumbles can transform the outcome. Established retailers are advantaged by incumbency but are handicapped by their fear of cannibalization and their unwillingness to abandon the comfortable annuities of the past. Suppliers tend to see only upside from an opportunity to end-run the retailer and reach the consumer directly: they discount the danger that new electronic retailers and navigators will prove as powerful and aggressive as today's category-killing physical retailers. The new players themselves bring nothing special to the party except a willingness to embrace new technology and take risks, but they believe, rightly or wrongly, that they can outsmart and outrun the lumbering competition. These new players can quickly become incumbents themselves and can repeat the errors of their victims: the deconstructor can be deconstructed. New players can also serve as powerful allies in enabling established players to settle old scores with each other: they can become kingmakers in the continuing battle between supplier and retailer.

Hierarchical Search

The power balance between suppliers, physical retailers, and the consumer is shaped in today's world by hierarchical structures of information. On the supply side, the bonding of information flows to physical flows implies hierarchical relations among suppliers, wholesalers, and retailers. On the demand side, constraints on richness and reach force the consumer into a hierarchical pattern of search and choice. The two hierarchical structures mirror and sustain each other.

For the consumer, the inefficiency of hierarchical search makes for difficult, and often bad, choices. For the supplier, being subordinated hierarchically to the retailer blocks opportunities to build a relationship with the consumer and often puts the supplier at the mercy of the retailer. Conversely, for the retailer control of the choke point in the flow of information between supplier and consumer is the source of a large proportion of competitive advantage. Any business logic that eliminates such choke points offers huge threats and opportunities to all the participants.

At its most fundamental level, searching in a hierarchy means crawling along the richness/reach trade-off (see Figure 6-1). The consumer starts with a wide range of options but limited rich information about each. He then makes a series of choices. At each step, he reduces the number of options to obtain richer information on those remaining— greater richness is gained as reach narrows. The impossibility of gathering rich information on the universe of choices in a cost-effective fashion compels the individual to search hierarchically for the product or service.

For example, if a man wants to buy a shirt, his first decision might be to choose a particular street or a shopping mall (see Figure 6-2). Second, he would have to decide which store to visit. Then he would have to find the shirt department.

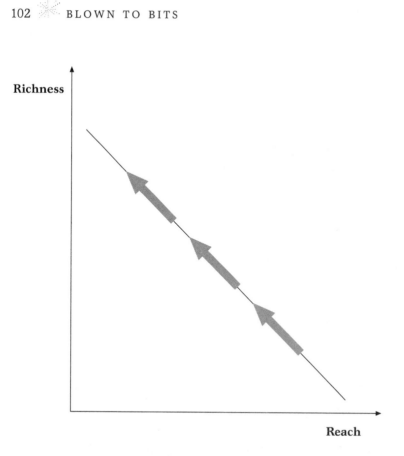

Richness

Reach

Figure 6-1: Hierarchical Search: Crawling along the Trade-off

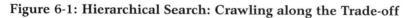

Then, depending on how the merchandise is laid out, he would search by brand and then collar size (or perhaps in the reverse order), and finally he would pick out the shirt itself. Each of these choices is constrained by the previous ones. If he wants to compare offerings across stores, he has to back up to the first level of this searching process and repeat it. That might mean driving somewhere else.

Of course, there are other ways to conduct the same search. The consumer might go into a shop and rely on a salesperson's recommendation. Or he might pick a catalog and choose something. But the choices, in their different ways, are still hierarchical.

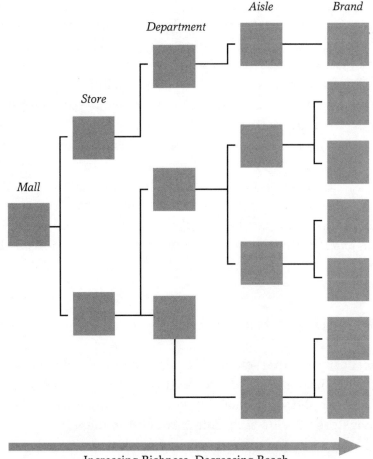

Increasing Richness, Decreasing Reach

Source: Adapted from Philip B. Evans and Thomas S. Wurster, "Strategy and the New Economics of Information," *Harvard Business Review,* September–October 1997, p. 75.

Figure 6-2: Hierarchical Search: Buying a Shirt in a Mall

Hierarchical search imposes costs on the buyer. The most obvious are the time and effort required to conduct a search with any measure of completeness. It is exhausting to be exhaustive, and people rarely do it. Instead of conducting a comprehensive search, people search along a path familiar from previous searches that produced a satisfactory out-come. They may rely on serendipitous guidance from some-one (a salesman) or something (a promotional display) that they discover along the way.

These shortcuts impose a more insidious cost: unin-formed choice. In a hierarchy, buyers—and searchers of all types, for that matter—are obliged to make decisions based on incomplete information. As a result, they act with *bounded rationality*: they make decisions that are sensible given the incomplete information that they possess and the high cost of getting better information. They settle for a choice that may not be exactly what they want but seems *good enough*. But they would make different decisions if they really knew all the alternatives.[2]

Navigating a Hierarchy

The cost and inefficiency of hierarchical choice, together with the importance of the final selection to buyers and to sellers, implies a critical intermediary function: *navigation*. Navigators provide shortcuts through the maze.

Navigation is critical to many businesses. In some instances, navigation may be a business in its own right (the Yellow Pages, a personal shopper, or an independent finan-cial adviser). Often, it is a function within a business (the White Pages, a salesperson, or a stockbroker).[3] Film review-ers and restaurant guides are navigators. So are human advisers, agents, or consultants who work for the buyer, the seller, or as middlemen. Market makers that connect buyers and sellers are navigators. Advertisements, brands, a sales pitch, shop windows, and store layouts all serve navigational functions.

Some navigators serve the interests of buyers by expanding and comparing the choices available. Others serve the interests of sellers by guiding buyers to the seller's products, preferably those with higher margins. And there are multiple sellers: the supplier who originates the product may convey one set of navigational messages through advertising and product brochures, but the layout of the retail environment and the guidance proffered by the salesperson may reflect the retailer's very different set of navigational priorities. No intelligent seller's navigator ignores the interests of the buyer, but he or she (or it) will aim to maximize the interests of the navigator's owner while providing the buyer with a product or service that is *good enough*.

The Seller's Advantage

Sellers dominate the navigation process. Since sellers (whether suppliers or retailers) are generally larger than buyers, they enjoy greater economies of scale in marketing than buyers do in searching. They can afford to devote much more careful thought to influencing the buying decision than buyers might ever want to expend on making it. They invest enormous sums in advertising, image development, and brand promotion to encourage consumers to start their hierarchical search at certain points and to make certain critical choices. They employ *push-based* marketing techniques—the salesman's personal pitch, the promotion of particular products, shelf layouts—to grab the consumer's attention and influence her behavior favorably. They exploit the fact that once they have sold one product, it is cheap and relatively easy to promote and sell others, at the time of purchase or subsequently. Push-based marketing works precisely because of the cost to consumers of backing up through the search hierarchy: having expended time and effort to get to this point, they are unwilling to retrace their steps. Suppliers who are excluded from access to this critical choke point are forced to rely on high-reach/low-richness means, such as advertising, or peripherally influencing consumers' decisions.

Inefficiencies of the hierarchical search process are the foundation of many of the competitive advantages of sellers today. These advantages include cross-selling, the control of a high-traffic channel, the ownership of a strong umbrella brand, the value of an effective sales force, and the power of a customer franchise. In fact, the only supplier advantages really excluded are ones specific to the product itself—cost, features, and technology. The only retailer advantages excluded from the search process are those related to physical distribution—logistics, inventory turns, and location. Just about every other source of competitive advantage for sellers depends on the hierarchical structure of consumer choice.

But the advent of universal, rich connectivity blows all this to bits. Many of the competitive advantages that had required high searching and switching costs, limited choice, and information asymmetries become unsustainable. The profitability that flowed from these advantages dries up.

Reach without Navigation

The number of cereal brands in the average supermarket has multiplied in the past twenty years, yet the market share of the leading brands has gone up. Why? Because the consumer has no means of navigating the visual cacophony of the cereal shelf. Faced with infinite choice, consumers suffer from infinite confusion, and therefore fall back on the tried and true. There are numerous categories where leading brands have *gained* from the proliferation of alternatives, because infinite choice without navigation amounts to nothing more than clutter.[4]

As anybody who has attempted a search and has found four thousand "hits" will testify, the World Wide Web is in much the same situation. Reach has exploded beyond anybody's ability to navigate it. That results in the "Corn Flakes" phenomenon: a few high-profile brands have risen above the clutter and enjoy a high measure of loyalty and stickiness, precisely because people have no interest in wrestling with all the alternatives. Amazon.com derives 63 percent of its revenue from repeat customers.[5] The technology of "favorites" or "bookmarks" reinforces the propensity to use high profile brands as instruments of navigation.

However, there is nothing inherent in the medium that necessitates this stickiness. Quite the converse: alternatives are but a click away. *Stickiness is a consequence of the undeveloped state of navigation.* And the medium is inherently predisposed to navigation because its whole architecture is based on connectivity and standards. But navigation will evolve not because it is technically possible or because it is trendy. It will evolve because businesses will find they can achieve competitive advantage by providing a way for parties to find each other in the face of nearly infinite choice.

A New World of Navigation

Separating the economics of information from the economics of things allows the navigation function to become totally independent of the physical processes of distribution and fulfillment. The new navigators can guide people and help parties find each other, but they do not need also to serve as physical distributors in the way that a retailer does. They do

A Brave New World of Navigation

When navigation corresponds to physical functions, sellers (whether originators of the physical product or the physical distributors we call retailers) can influence how consumers navigate and choose products and services. But when the economics of information and the economics of things separate, the search universe no longer needs to relate to the physically defined producer and distributor industries. There is no longer any reason for the physically defined industries to enjoy *any* privileged position in influencing consumer choice. It is impossible to overemphasize the importance of this. If navigation drives a large portion of competitive advantage, and navigation is recast as a separate entity, then the existing business loses control of a main source of profit.

This brave new world makes the following possible:

- **Abundant connectivity.** Every participant can directly establish an information connection with every other participant without any third member blocking or controlling that connection.

- **Common information standards.** The richness/reach trade-off gets blown up through connectivity and standards. Navigators create the standards. They not only provide the basics, such as security and reliability, but also make it possible for industries and other specialty groups with unique languages to "talk" digitally about everything from personal finance to the color and texture of fabrics.

- **Infinite choice.** The universe of searchable rich options explodes. This *increases* the need for navigators. But these navigators add value by facilitating choice, not by controlling some choke point in the search process. There are no choke points.

- **Negligible searching and switching costs.** Enabled by connectivity and standards, participants can link and unlink without significant constraint or cost.

- **Fluidity.** The same task or function can be achieved through a variety of different combinations of participants. No one combination is necessarily the best combination. And no one combination is necessarily a lasting combination. Indeed, the participants are constantly combining, separating, and recombining.

- **Lack of a center.** Nobody controls or directs, and there is no hub. Each participant pursues its own goals and follows its own rules, and the system coheres.

- **Adaptability.** Modularity, lack of a center, and the possibility of rapid combination and recombination create an exceptionally adaptable system—one that is more akin to an ecosystem than a traditionally engineered system.

not even need to be parties to the transaction: they can be "agents" instead of principals. Their function can be to point out the best choice (from someone's point of view) without taking any responsibility for its delivery. The possibility of navigation independent of physical flows immediately puts the supplier back on an equal footing with the retailer. It also allows an electronic retailer, the consumer, or some agent operating on the consumer's behalf to perform aspects of the navigation function. The physical underpinnings of the choke point are removed.

As purely informational functions, the new navigators can exploit the shifting trade-off between richness and reach. Unconstrained by reach, they can offer *all* alternatives to *all* searchers simultaneously. Unconstrained by richness, they can offer as much detail, with whatever order, presentation, or emphasis their client prefers. Navigators can costlessly and seamlessly ally with each other to present richer, more comprehensive information collectively than they could separately.

But who is this new navigator? Is it a business in its own right, like Yahoo!? Is it a piece of software operating as an agent, like Quicken? An electronic retailer like Amazon.com? Is it perhaps not a business at all, but a function? Something the consumer does? An electronic front end offered by a conventional physical retailer? Or by a product supplier?

The answer today is "all of the above." But that is to be expected in the early days of any competitive convulsion. On the Web today, every possible approach is being tried by somebody, somewhere. Navigation will eventually stabilize, and the stabilizing principle will be competitive advantage.

The new navigators will compete on three dimensions: *reach, agency affiliation,* and *richness* (see Figure 6-3). *Reach,* for a navigator, means the size of the universe across which it can navigate. The bigger the better. *Agency affiliation* means the closeness with which the navigator identifies with the interests of its client(s) (who may be any combination of consumers, retailers, and suppliers) and serves as an agent for the clients' interests. *Richness* means the quality and customization of the information that the navigator delivers.

Competing on Reach

There are approximately five thousand bookstores in the United States, and on average each carries about eighty thousand titles.[6] The largest physical bookstore in the United States carries 175,000 titles. Amazon.com offers *three million* volumes and is "located" on some twenty-five million com-

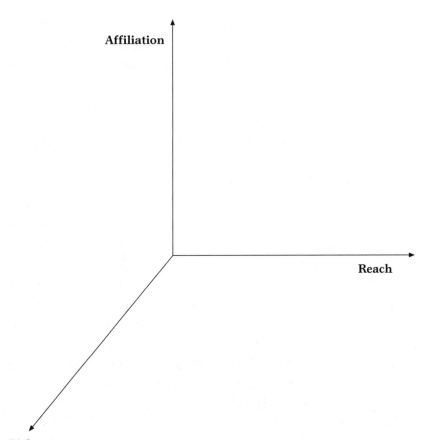

Figure 6-3: The Three Dimensions of Competitive Advantage for Navigators

puter screens. This orders-of-magnitude jump in reach is possible precisely because the navigation function (catalog) is separated from the physical function (inventory). The average computer superstore displays about twenty PC configurations. By letting the consumer permutate hardware components, Dell's Internet site offers over ten million configurations.[7] The average music superstore carries fifty thousand titles; CDNOW is so confident of its reach that it will give two free CDs to any customer who can find a single title that is missing from its catalog. Unconstrained by physical limitations, reach explodes.

If reach matters to the consumer, then the navigator with greatest reach is advantaged, all else being equal.[8] Internet search engines such as Yahoo! and Excite compete (among other things) on how much of the World Wide Web they have indexed. Search engines that are losing the race for reach merge with each other in order to stay abreast of the leaders. Barnesandnoble.com combined forces with Books Online by Bertelsmann to top Amazon with a catalog of 4.6 million book titles. (Whether the extra 1.6 million alternatives matter to even the most avid reader is a matter of conjecture.)

Bob Metcalfe, inventor of Ethernet and one of the most perceptive students of the information revolution, first observed that the value of a network is proportional to the square of the number of people using it. The value to any one individual of a telephone or fax machine, for instance, is proportional to the number of friends and associates who have phones or faxes. Double the number of participants, therefore, and the value *to each participant* is doubled, and the total value of the network is multiplied fourfold.[9]

Two-way navigation follows Metcalfe's Law. On-line classifieds, for example, are a navigation business where buyers and sellers are looking for each other. Buyers choose where to browse based on the number of advertisers, and sellers select where to advertise based on the number of browsers. Whoever establishes a clear lead becomes the first choice for buyers looking to reach the maximum number of sellers, and also for sellers seeking the maximum number of buyers. Reach then becomes a self-fulfilling prophecy. Whoever has superior share gains share. In the on-line automotive classified business, there is a race between Auto Trader and Microsoft's CarPoint to reach a million on-line vehicle listings. Both competitors understand the value of being the highest-reach navigator in a network-based business. Once one competitor establishes a strong lead, it is not clear that anybody would then be interested in the *second* choice.[10]

In many navigation businesses, a high reach navigator would be of great value to consumers, but none yet exists. A "wine" navigator to every vintage for every label; a "durable goods" navigator that provides comprehensive comparisons across the bewildering arrays of products, options, and features; a navigator to all long-distance phone plans or to all job openings for librarians—it is easy to conceive of dozens of businesses that would be enormously valuable to consumers and competitively advantaged by merit of the network effect. But consumer value emerges only when the *absolute* size of the navigational domain passes some critical threshold. And, in each of these possible businesses, no navigator has yet reached that point.

Critical Mass

This poses a central strategic challenge for navigators: building critical mass. If reach begets reach, as it does in so many cases, the first competitor to achieve some threshold level of critical mass will take off. All the others, absent some other way to compete (i.e., affiliation or richness), fall back into eventual oblivion. Navigators should *quite rationally* cut price, give the product away, and merge with their competitors to beat everyone else to that magic threshold. Hence the browser wars and stock market valuations that place greater value on reach than they do on profits.

Hence also the willingness, often the necessity, for players, even competitors, to pool their interests in order to achieve a critical mass collectively that is inaccessible to each acting in isolation. Six leading American newspapers are collaborating on a joint venture called CareerPath.com to offer nationwide electronic job classifieds for higher-skill employment. Aware that none could achieve critical mass starting from its localized market position, and fearful that an outsider like Microsoft might otherwise beat them to critical mass, these companies have forsworn control, brand, and a piece of their identity in pursuit of reach.[11]

The measure of reach and the level of reach that constitutes critical mass both depend on the search domain: the universe of relevant alternatives *as defined by the searcher.* The search domain for unskilled jobs is likely to be specific to a locality but nonspecific with respect to job categories. The search domain for high-skill jobs is likely to be the exact reverse: specific to the skill but open, quite possibly, to relocation options. Electronic classified businesses for the former are therefore likely to be segmented by geography, but within each region, one player should dominate. Navigators for the latter are likely to be national, but finely segmented by job category. The local newspaper stands a good chance of dominating the former. But who is best equipped to achieve critical mass in the latter? Who has the most comprehensive reach to librarians? A nationwide consortium of newspapers? Or is it perhaps the American Library Association? When the physical barriers to navigating cease to matter (such as owning a printing press), advantage in building critical mass can emerge in some surprising places. The fact that a nationwide consortium of newspapers covers fifty job classifications could be quite irrelevant to the searcher who cares about only one. Critical mass depends not on absolute numbers, but on reach *relative to the domain of search.*

The Competitive Struggle

From the point of view of the insurgent (the new navigator), getting to this critical mass is the principal challenge. The most spectacular single example of electronic retailing is in the slightly unlikely category of books. The reason is that a wide-reaching product list already existed, maintained by the wholesalers for the benefit of independent bookshops. By negotiating access to that database, Amazon.com was able to jump-start an initial offering of over a million books: instant critical mass. If Amazon had needed to sign up each publisher individually, the story would have been profoundly different.

Incumbents have a lot to lose. Traditional (physical) retailers fear the rise of the electronic retailer with superior reach. Product suppliers and traditional retailers alike fear the rise of the agent navigator who facilitates broad-reaching comparisons without even being party to the transaction. However, a component of critical mass for either kind of new navigator is often the incumbents' product information, price lists, and willingness to accept business switched through that navigator. This opens the possibility of *denying critical mass*. If enough suppliers refuse to sell through the e-retailer, or enough retailers refuse to provide information to the dispassionate agent, neither the e-retailer nor the agent can achieve critical mass.

Certainly that is what is blocking the realization of many businesses that might spring from armchair conceptualizing. But herein lies a crucial subtlety. As a simple corollary of the separation of the economics of information from the economics of things, *the domain of search that defines critical mass bears no necessary relation to the domains of the physical supplier or distribution industries*. The critical mass in question

From Your Perspective

If You Are a "Category Killer" Retailer . . .

- You have been winning the "reach" game in physical space (against department stores and general merchandisers) through overwhelming selection and your mastery of logistics. But that is all economics of things. You will lose the reach game in informational space *if* direct fulfillment is a serious alternative to your current distribution system. In a lot of categories, it is.

- You will be attacked by your suppliers and by electronic retailers simultaneously. Do not presume that past success indicates future impregnability.

- If you are going to be attacked, even in small slivers of your business, do it to yourself before somebody does it to you. And understand the multiplicative effects that even slight erosion can have on the profitability of a high-fixed-cost business.

- Your key advantage is your unique ability to combine local and virtual presence into a single integrated retailing position. Your challenge is to realize the synergies between the two formats without letting fear of cannibalization limit the competitiveness of the latter.

If You Are a Product Supplier . . .

- Reach for you is a two-edged sword: it might enable you to escape the bear hug of your retailers, but it simultaneously exposes you to new navigators whose reach is potentially far greater than yours. You *could* end up back where you started, beholden to an electronic version of Wal-Mart. Or, if you do it right, you could end up winning in a big way.

- If you have a better mousetrap, the explosion of reach and the rise of navigators are a blessing: the navigators will prepare a pathway to your door.

- But if your mousetrap is much the same as everyone else's, those same navigators will subject you to an unwelcome level of comprehensive comparison.

- Understand that competing effectively on navigation and reach requires a set of skills that most product suppliers totally lack. Aggressively add these skills, or risk failure.

If You Are an Electronic Retailer . . .

- Recognize that reach is the Achilles' heel of the product supplier, and go after it aggressively. Do not sacrifice your biggest advantage for the limited benefits of a few exclusive deals.

- Don't look at your business through traditional retailing concepts and metrics. Most generalizations about consumer virtual shopping become invalid within a year.

- Beware of the "Category Killers." Their only real handicap is their unwillingness to take you seriously.

may not relate to the incumbents' business at all. Somebody may create a navigator business that achieves critical mass in some apparently unrelated business *and then migrate across categories.* Microsoft has done this repeatedly within the software industry. Amazon, having built a brand franchise by appropriating the critical mass in somebody else's product catalog, is now playing Metcalfe's network game in the reverse direction: using all those book buyers as the buyer network for new product offerings in successive retail categories. Since Amazon's product offering has no necessary connection with physical economics (it could always out-source fulfillment), it is quite opaque at this stage what, if anything, sets the bounds of its business. Once a navigator establishes critical mass in *some* informational domain, it is a totally open question how far the business can be extended.

This leads to two fundamental propositions about reach:

- Critical mass is a precondition for value creation, but there is no guarantee that it will be achieved.

- Critical mass is relative to a domain defined by the economics of information, not by the economics of things.

Many half-hearted, first-generation strategies for electronic commerce pursued by product suppliers or traditional retailers stem directly from failure to take these two propositions seriously.

Product suppliers often see electronic commerce as an opportunity to build a "direct-to-consumer" relationship: a chance finally to turn the tables on retailers who have used their lock on the consumer to put relentless pressure on supplier margins. They try to do so discreetly, of course, since the retailer is still their primary customer, but the hope is to build at least a back channel for communication with the consumer, and perhaps some direct distribution, and thereby tilt bargaining power back in their direction. The resulting offering is profoundly compromised: lots of brochure-like detail on the supplier's own product line, referrals to retailers for actual sales, or direct sales, perhaps, under terms calculated to cause the retailer no offense.

Traditional retailers are even more compromised, caught between product suppliers eager to bypass them and the new navigators, both the electronic retailers and the navigational agents. They undertake a defensive strategy: creating an electronic presence to draw traffic to their shops, but with no serious intention of cannibalizing their current physical infrastructure. They avoid any comprehensive navigational offering, even to the content of their own stores, because they want to force the consumer to navigate by coming to the store and walking the aisles. They tend to focus instead on promotions, bargains of the day, traffic builders. It is interesting to observe that there is *not a single example* of an established physical retailer actually taking the lead in electronic retailing in its category.

Both product suppliers and traditional retailers often fail to exploit the new economics of information: they offer no real increase in reach, they define scope and therefore critical mass in terms of their own physical economics, and they offer little that the consumer has much reason to value. They focus even less on *relative* reach: relative, that is, to the insurgent navigators. Small wonder that the results are so unimpressive.

But the biggest danger is not unimpressive results. The biggest danger is the obvious consequence of insurgents pursuing critical mass while incumbents do not; at some point, precisely because they have been given a free hand, the insurgents will achieve it.

Second-generation strategy for incumbents starts with the recognition that reach is critical to survival. Product suppliers playing to win need to grasp that what may feel like a quantum leap in reach for them is often quite inadequate relative to the reach of the insurgent navigator. Suppliers need to focus on reach within a *consumer-defined* domain of search, emulating the way the insurgent defines his business. The navigational metaphor becomes *solving a consumer problem*, not touting a product brochure. If that necessitates more products than the supplier makes, then he builds the requisite reach through alliances with complementary suppliers. And if reach to competitors is an essential part of navigational value, then competing suppliers must find a neutral (and legal) way of making that possible before some outsider does it to them. Physical distribution needs to be handled in the lowest-cost way, whatever the consequences for the current infrastructure of distributors and retailers. In some cases, such as PCs and cars, the least-cost logistical chain is manufacture-to-order, which can make the supplier who sells direct cheaper than even the most efficient electronic retailer. By combining these stratagems, the product supplier may never equal the reach of the electronic navigator, but if he can stay *close enough*, then there are plenty of other dimensions on which to compete, as we will see in the following chapters.

Similarly, the traditional retailer pursuing a second-generation strategy ought to be able to compete with extraordinary effectiveness against the upstarts *if* this retailer is willing to run her electronic retailing business as a serious, and largely independent, operation. She can match anybody in product reach. She has obvious purchasing synergies between the physical and the electronic operations. There may be com-

---

Frequently Asked Questions

1. **Does the importance of critical mass mean that the first entrant always wins?**

   No. Latecomers can carve out and dominate segments that fit better into the search domains that some group of consumers really wants. These could cut across the terrain dominated by the first entrants, or they could be pockets within that terrain. But in the latter case, the latecomers would have to outperform the first entrants on affiliation or richness (and the first entrants, knowing this, are not standing still).

2. **Which types of businesses will universal, far-reaching connectivity and rich information standards affect most?**

   Businesses where the richness/reach trade-off is shifting *and* some embedded compromises in customer value are thereby abolished.

3. **Is reach more important than agency affiliation or richness?**

   The explosion in reach will initially have the biggest and most visible impact on changing the *shape* of businesses in the future. But affiliation and richness will often prove more powerful over the long term as sources of competitive advantage and therefore profitability.

4. **What capabilities should I try to develop to capitalize on enhanced reach?**

   Enhanced reach requires that you develop effective ways of dealing directly with your end consumers. Put yourself in the mindset of the new navigator—see the consumer through his eyes. This may mean developing a whole host of new capabilities, particularly if you are a product supplier, one step removed from your end consumer.

monalities in logistics, although that is not self-evident: an efficient system for delivery to the home is often quite different from that required for replenishing shelves. Merchandising skills may be transferable, or they may prove deceptively different. Brand, if it has any value in the physical world, will generally be transferable. Local physical presence may provide a basis for customer services that the electronic retailer cannot match.

All that is required, of both product supplier and traditional retailer, is recognition that if cannibalization is going to happen anyway, it is much better to do it to oneself.

As the sheer volume of information and commerce moving over the Web grows, as the limitations of first-generation strategies become more apparent, as the prospects of replicating the strategies of the first-generation heroes dim, and as the laws of competitive advantage become better understood, it is entirely predictable that reach will become the fulcrum of an altogether more intense competitive struggle, and that self-cannibalization will be accepted by incumbents as inevitable. In the case of Britannica, or, for that matter, Barnes and Noble, the point is obvious in retrospect. The challenge, emotional as well as intellectual, is to see it prospectively.

SOUND BITS

- The new navigators compete against each other on reach, affiliation, and richness. This competitive dynamic has no necessary connection to the physically defined ways that traditional navigators compete.

- The greatest benefit from e-commerce is the explosion of reach, but reach is mere clutter without navigation.

- "Push" (e.g., push-based marketing, selling, and distribution) is a corollary of high search costs. Reduce those costs, and "push" gives way to "pull."

- "Stickiness" is likely to be transitory: it occurs only because reach has developed faster than navigation. Never presume that you have created an electronic annuity.

- Random, small-scale innovation may never achieve critical mass. First-generation strategies of experimentation will give way to second-generation strategies of big bets.

7

competing on affiliation

NEW NAVIGATORS DERIVE much of their advantage—versus the established players and versus each other—by affiliating as closely as possible with the interests of the consumer. This tilt toward consumers is a direct and fundamental consequence of the blowup of the richness/reach trade-off. The greater the reach of navigators across suppliers, and the more intense the competition among navigators for the loyalty and attention of consumers, the weaker is the navigators' bond to any one seller and the greater is the pressure on them to serve as buyers' rather then sellers' agents. This tilt in affiliation shifts the balance of power from sellers toward buyers.

From the product suppliers' point of view, the tilt in affiliation threatens their influence over the buying process. This tilt also threatens the effectiveness of their substantial investments to control retail channels and patterns of consumer choice. The emergence of new navigation channels outside their control poses acute dilemmas for those they do control:

whether to keep them strictly loyal at the price of long-term competitiveness, or preserve their competitiveness by sacrificing some of their efficacy as captive channels. Product suppliers have to choose between adjusting to the reality of buyer-affiliated navigators and trying to prevent the shift in agency affiliation from occurring.

The affiliation of retailers is more complex and more ambiguous than that of suppliers. Retailers by definition buy from suppliers and then resell to consumers: in some ways they represent consumer interests to product suppliers (negotiating for high quality and low price), and in others, they represent supplier interests to consumers (cooperative advertising and joint promotions). Retailers vary in their mix of these two roles.

All retailers welcome the cooperative advertising, promotional materials, tie-ins, and sales support offered by their suppliers. Nike's large force of sales evangelists, called "Ekins" ("Nike" spelled backward), train retailers' salespeople to explain shoe technology to customers and guide them to the most appropriately designed (Nike) shoe. Detail men from packaged goods companies rearrange their products in supermarkets to maximize the banner effect of shelf space and navigate customers toward the current promotion. Apple Computer manages its value-added resellers as extensions of its own sales force. Retailers whose physical economics constrain them to a narrow range of suppliers (such as motorcycle dealers or camera shops) are passionate advocates of the offerings from their preferred suppliers.

However, not all retailers are so closely aligned with sellers. Hard goods and packaged goods suppliers certainly don't see Wal-Mart as an extension of their sales forces. They are much more likely to think of Wal-Mart as a (or *the*) customer. And while they have little choice but to collaborate with Wal-Mart, they would hardly characterize the relationship as one driven by an overwhelming commonality of interests. Indeed, by pressing relentlessly for maximum choice and everyday low prices and by actively discouraging suppliers from spending money on self-serving forms of promotion, Wal-Mart, supermarket chains, and category killers affiliate themselves much more closely with the consumer than with the supplier. To be more precise, they affiliate themselves with the *collective* rather than the *individual* interests of consumers; they are still mass retailers.

For retailers with close ties to particular suppliers, the tilt in affiliation raises questions about the continuing viability of their strategy. For retailers without such close ties (such as general merchandisers and category killers), it presents the opportunity, indeed often the imperative, to position even more aggressively as champion of the consumer.

The Affiliation Spectrum

"Affiliation" does not mean caring for the customer: any supplier, retailer, or navigator has to do that. It does not refer to any of the helpful, positive-sum activities by which sellers further their own interests by furthering those of their customers. That is simply good business. The test of affiliation is where the consumer's gain is the seller's loss. Informing the consumer of purchasing alternatives available from other suppliers; explaining why a premium feature is not worth the money; sharing unflattering information on product performance or customer satisfaction: these are the kinds of navigational services that consumers would expect from a navigator serving their interests. They rarely get it, because it is not the purpose of most navigators to serve the interests of consumers. The purpose of most navigators is to serve the interests of sellers.

This is obviously true of advertising, product brochures, and sales pitches, which the seller pays for, creates, and controls. It is equally though less obviously true for intermediaries who facilitate or broker transactions among others, such as insurance agents, home decorators, and securities brokers. Whenever such an intermediary gets paid by the seller, it is a reasonable bet that the intermediary pursues the seller's interests.[1]

Some independent navigators flourish by maintaining a studied ambiguity as to where their affiliation really lies. Computer and stereo magazines offer extensive reviews of hardware and software products. But more than 80 percent of their revenue typically comes from advertising placed by the suppliers of those products. These magazines do not want to offend a major advertiser by panning its latest product, but neither do they want to compromise the objectivity that their readers expect. Hence a delicate balancing act: rigorous lab tests, uncritical gushing about the latest in industry technology, and a general reluctance to be really trenchant about anything. Newspapers and newsmagazines resolve the same ambiguity by segregating the editorial and business sides of the organization.

Exclusively buyer-affiliated navigation is the exception. *Consumer Reports* provides technical product evaluations, carries no advertising, and assiduously avoids association with any seller. Readers have to pay $2.95 for a thirty-page issue, far more per page of text than the cost of advertising-sponsored equivalents. Some human navigators are buyer-affiliated. Architects often deal with contractors on behalf of the customer in return for a fixed percentage of the project cost. In the corporate sphere, insurance brokers work unambiguously for their corporate clients to evaluate property and casualty risks and to buy insurance on their behalf. Purchasing departments navigate through sourcing options with an expertise (and aggressiveness) that the rest of the organization could never hope to muster. But in every case, if customers want a buyer-affiliated navigator, they have to be willing to pay for it.

The Logic of Affiliation

There are two reasons why navigators affiliate with sellers. One is the fact that rich navigation tends to be *specific* to suppliers. The other is the unwillingness of consumers to pay for navigation.

A salesman with only one product to sell (such as an encyclopedia) and with thousands of potential customers is going to push that product as if his life depended on it. Similarly, a purchasing agent, serving one encyclopedia publishing company and dealing with a large universe of printers, will rigorously protect that publisher's interests. The salesman or purchasing agent does not have to be employed by the corporation for these affiliations to apply: they follow from the logic of *specificity*. With narrow reach and few other options, both parties become highly dependent on each other, and there are no conflicts of interest for the navigator's loyalty. Specificity—the extent to which the navigator's economics depend on the economics of the sellers or buyers with whom he is tied—drives a large part of affiliation. The employment relation between the company and its salesman or purchasing agent is then a *consequence* of the affiliation, not really a cause.[2]

In a navigational context, specificity is determined by reach. A navigator positioned to assist an early choice in the consumer's navigational hierarchy may have rich knowledge of the searcher (a customizable search agent or personal adviser, for example) and certainly will have low-richness/high-reach knowledge of the domain being searched (directories, product lists, phone numbers). That makes the navigator *possibly* specific to the consumer but certainly *not* specific to any individual seller in the domain being searched. Therefore, the navigator is likely to be affiliated with the interests of the consumer. A navigator in the middle of a search hierarchy, with high reach and low richness connections to both buyers and sellers (such as a newspaper classified section), will be neutral between the two principal parties. A navigator positioned to support a *late* choice in a consumer's search hierarchy, where the search has been narrowed to a just few alternatives (such as a salesman), is unlikely to have rich knowledge of the consumer who has found his way to him. But he is very likely to be in the business of offering rich knowledge of the narrow domain of choice that he covers. That makes such a navigator nonspecific to the consumer but very specific to the supplier or suppliers whose products or services are being searched. Therefore, such a navigator is very likely to be formally or informally affiliated with these suppliers. That is why, in the world of the richness/reach trade-off, navigators closely affiliated with suppliers provide the vast majority of the detailed, rich navigation.

This has an important implication. If reach controls specificity and specificity controls affiliation, *the same constraints that limit reach also control agency affiliation.* If it is only because of limited reach that navigator specificity arises, then anything that blows up the trade-off between richness and reach not only undermines the necessity for hierarchical search, it also simultaneously undermines the logic for navigators affiliating with sellers. *A shift away from seller affiliation becomes possible once the trade-off between richness and reach blows up.*

Paying for Navigation

The shift in affiliation becomes possible, but not inevitable. There are numerous examples of navigators covering the same domains, and therefore operating with the same reach, but behaving differently as a consequence of being paid differently. "Financial advisers," for example, can be salespeople employed and paid by brokerage houses to sell securities, or they can be independent counselors paid an hourly advisory fee by the customer. Some home decorators receive a 40 percent commission from the furniture shop (a number rarely admitted to the customer), others bill their clients at an hourly rate like architects. The White Pages and the Yellow Pages have roughly the same navigational reach, but one is paid for as part of the phone bill and the other is an advertising medium. In each case, and quite independent of reach, the options that the navigator presents, and the quality and tone of the guidance that he, she, or it provides, are subtly or not so subtly influenced by the navigator's economics. So even if reach explodes and new navigation models become possible, the affiliation of the navigation function still critically depends on how it is paid for.

However, in a world unconstrained by richness and reach, navigation becomes orders of magnitude *cheaper*. When all information sources can be accessed electronically, when any item of information has to be collected only once, when standards spread through the self-organizing logic of networks, and when navigators can navigate to and through each other, stunningly sophisticated searches become possible for fractions of a cent. And both the cost and the capability of such searches will continue to be driven by Moore's Law.

The sheer cheapness of navigation in the electronic domain changes the nature of the problem. The choice between a salesman paid for by the seller and a consultant paid for by the buyer is a real dilemma, but it is finessed when many of those functions can be performed electronically for pennies. Internet search engines provide navigational services without charging the customer. This makes sense given the low cost of the electronic product: it is simply *so cheap* to provide electronic navigation that a bit of banner advertising, pennies for a hyperlink, or some minor collateral benefit suffices to justify the whole navigator service. Navigator economics in the world of pure information are quite different from those embedded in the economics of people and things. The navigator does not have to be affiliated with a seller to justify giving away its services.

Fundamentally, as search increases in richness and reach and simultaneously drops in cost, the search function becomes less and less dependent on a high level of assistance from a few suppliers and more reliant on less involvement (banner advertising, hyperlinks) from many suppliers. This implies an affiliation shift: the navigator will have some loyalty to its advertisers as a group, but not to any particular advertiser: there are simply too many. The navigator is forced to be largely dispassionate because of its *reach*.

But this statement dodges the issue a bit. High-quality navigation may well cost real money and may well be economically feasible only if customers are willing to pay. Much of the customers' unwillingness to pay may stem from the fact that today they don't have to, and it is difficult for them to distinguish quality that is worth the premium. With time, as the Wild West character of cyberspace subsides, that may change. Branded navigators, delivering quality content for a subscription, are likely to emerge. Wherever the outcome of a navigational process matters to consumers and whenever information becomes sufficiently symmetric to make that value manifest, the logic of value pricing is likely to emerge.

The Competitive Advantage of Navigators

This leads to the fundamental principle that will govern the competitive evolution of navigation. When navigators are constrained in terms of reach, they connect to each other hierarchically, and those navigators providing high-richness/low-reach information become affiliated, formally or informally, with sellers. This is undesirable from the consumer's point of view, but consumers have no alternative unless they are willing to pay the substantial cost of their own navigator.

Once the richness/reach trade-off is broken, however, navigators cease to be specific to sellers and in many contexts become very cheap. This leads navigators to compete with each other for the attention of consumers based on two new factors: reach and affiliation with consumer interests. They *can* compete that way because the reach and therefore specificity constraints have been relaxed; they *will* compete that way because that is how consumers prefer to choose among navigators. The pursuit of competitive advantage among navigators should, therefore, drive them toward higher reach and closer affiliation with customer interests. Indeed, if reach is subject to the network economics of Metcalfe's Law, navigators will dash for the northeast corner of Figure 6-3 with an intensity driven by the knowledge that winner takes all. A potential big winner in this scenario is the navigator who offers infinite reach and close affiliation with the consumer. The cyber equivalent of Wal-Mart.

The parallel makes a telling point. Wal-Mart did not set out to establish a close affiliation with consumer interests as its primary competitive advantage. Compared with many retailers, it is *not* particularly close to its customers. Wal-Mart's primary competitive advantage lies in physical economies: scale and logistics. These physical economies allow the retailer to offer wide selection, reaching many suppliers, which reduces the specificity of its supplier relationships. Those same physical economies give Wal-Mart enormous reach to millions of customers. Lack of specificity (dependence on any one supplier) plus customer volume give Wal-Mart the bargaining power to operate effectively as a consumer-affiliated intermediary by negotiating for lower prices and rapid delivery. Wal-Mart's segment is not necessarily one where consumer affiliation is of special value. Rather, it is the physical economics that enabled—and indeed caused—Wal-Mart to shift agency affiliation.

The same is true of the pure navigator business. Agency shifts occur not as a consequence of discovering latent customer needs for affiliated navigators, but rather as a consequence of the relaxing of the richness/reach constraints.

Implications for Sellers

For suppliers and for retailers this raises a troubling scenario. The trade-off between richness and reach blows up, enabling universal search to replace hierarchical search. Freed from their prior constraints, navigators compete against each other on reach and customer affiliation. Struggling to achieve critical mass, navigators push for reach, merge, and concentrate. As their reach goes up, their affiliation to sellers loosens, which proves a further advantage in competing for buyers. Some navigators get ahead of the others, cross the threshold of critical mass, and then march toward positions of monopoly in their respective search domains. Winner takes all. Armed with superior reach, a high level of consumer affiliation and trust, and equivalent richness (since by assumption the trade-off has been blown up), that navigator is advantaged in navigation against both retailers and suppliers. Retailers are demoted to the physical role of distributor. Suppliers see their business commoditized, or at least forced to compete on product-specific characteristics such as cost, technology, and features. Much of the value potential of the business is drained off. Just like what Wal-Mart did to the apparel business. Just like what Microsoft does to everybody.

Farfetched? Probably. It hasn't happened yet. In most businesses it will not happen. But it is a *logic*: a set of forces that compound the strategy calculations for all businesses. If a supplier or a retailer is to avoid that logic, there have to be some countervailing forces or strategies. In fact there are seven.

Continuation of the Richness/Reach Trade-off. The first line of defense is in areas where the existing richness/reach trade-off curve will endure. It is not clear, for example, how "streaming audio" technology will enable consumers remotely to select a pair of high-end stereo speakers or whether virtual reality technology will ever enable them to select a designer dress without trying it on. Although on-line apparel retailers now offer "virtual mannequins," customized to the size and appearance of the consumer, one might be skeptical that this will ever seriously replace fitting rooms. For these types of products, the economics of information and the economics of things are unlikely ever to separate; the richness/reach trade-off will therefore persist, and navigators (such as sales clerks) will continue to be affiliated with the seller.

This logic applies in specific slivers of navigation. Consumers can still develop a preliminary idea of what they want based on two-dimensional information, and after physical selection may still choose to find the lowest-priced, fastest-delivery supplier by a selection process unconstrained by richness and reach. As always, it is necessary to "deconstruct" a purchase quite minutely into its component

From Your Perspective

If You Are a New Navigator . . .

- Recognize that closer affiliation with consumers is a major competitive advantage for you. It is part of your Web identity. Cultivate it. Do not compromise consumer interests for your own short-term gain. Never do anything you would not want all your users to know about, because within a few days, they will.

If You Are a Product Supplier . . .

- Recognize that moving to a closer affiliation with your consumers is a profound shift in your business model.

- Understand that new navigators, who are more closely affiliated with your consumers, can effectively blunt the competitive advantages of your sales force, your advertising, or your product literature, almost overnight.

- Look seriously at alliances to address the affiliation problem: a *group* of suppliers may be able to create a navigator with strong customer affiliation that is more comprehensive and more credible than any of its members. Start from the search domain as defined by the consumer, identify the full range of desired content providers and the most compelling providers of credibility, then pick your alliance from that list.

If You Are a "Broad Reach" Retailer without Close Supplier Affiliations . . .

- As a general merchandiser or "category killer" you are better positioned than other established players (e.g., product suppliers, other narrow reach retailers) to build a navigational business based on reach and affiliation with the consumer. You have no commitment to particular suppliers. You do tough product evaluations anyway, and that is part of your brand. You have probably built your reputation on siding with the consumer. *You just have to be willing to cannibalize your current physical business.*

- The retailer best positioned to become the cyber-equivalent of Wal-Mart may be . . . Wal-Mart.

If You Are a "Narrow Reach" Retailer Closely Affiliated With a Few Suppliers . . .

- You are vulnerable. New navigators and "broad reach" retailers can beat you on reach and on consumer affiliation. Your suppliers may decide to make their case to consumers directly. Your real function is probably creating a shopping "experience." But how will it survive multimedia?

steps and consider the richness, reach, and affiliation logic of each separately. The fact that *one* step requires richness is not necessarily determining for the others.

Remember also that Moore's Law is steadily displacing the richness/reach trade-off. Wait ten years and information technology will be a hundred times more powerful. And the new technologies have no obligation to define richness in the same way as the old ones. Computer screens may never be able to match colors with the technical precision of offset printing (a question on which experts are currently divided), but sound and full-motion video may prove a more-than-adequate substitute for the purposes of electronic catalog shopping. It is easy to lapse into a definition of richness that reflects what delivery technologies are *currently* good at, rather than what the consumer in some fundamental sense really needs. Nonetheless, there are many arenas of choice where the richness/reach trade-off will not be displaced and where seller-affiliated navigators will continue to thrive.

Lack of Compromised Value. The second line of defense hinges on whether any value is actually released by the explosion of reach and the shift in agency affiliation. Does anybody need search engines, databases, threaded discussion groups, chat rooms—the whole panoply of comprehensive, objective navigation—to select and buy a pack of bubble gum? There are huge swaths of the economy where the value of superior navigation is simply not high enough. In many businesses, the mutual compromising of the economics of things and the economics of information, of richness and reach, is trivial.

However, trivial economics are a feather to every wind that blows. The fact that there is no particular reason to change them means that there is also no particular reason to preserve them. They could be transformed as the accidental consequence of apparently unrelated events. The destruction of the encyclopedia business can be interpreted—at least in part—as a casual byproduct of promotional economics in the computer industry. But that risk is hardly new. Many theoretically vulnerable businesses do perfectly well because neither competitors nor customers see enough value to warrant disrupting them.

Denial of Critical Mass. The third line of defense is altogether more strategic: take advantage of the *indeterminacy* of network evolution by preventing the new navigators from ever achieving critical mass. Suppliers and retailers are the source of the information on product features, price, and availability that the new navigators need. So simply refuse to make that information available. Let Yahoo! navigate to your Web site, but don't let it or anybody else parse your product lists and compare them with those of your competitor. If every seller does that, Yahoo! will be confined to its current role as a high-reach but low-richness navigator: a glorified phone directory.

There are two problems with this. The first is that technically it is quite difficult for a seller to stop a navigator from parsing information that the seller releases electronically. If customers can go to the Web site, so can navigators. It doesn't have to be a personal visit: technologies like Junglee enable a navigator to visit dozens of Web sites with the same inquiry, query them in whatever format each Web site requires, return the responses, and then parse and array the answers, all within a few seconds. Yahoo! uses Junglee technology to operate as a metanavigator, or navigator to navigators, for book buyers. Ask Yahoo! for a book and you get bids from some twenty electronic bookstores and can seamlessly choose the lowest price, the fastest delivery option. On average, this approach saves 5 percent to 10 percent of the price that one would pay by going to any one electronic bookstore. Amazon.com recently acquired Junglee. This will not stop metanavigators in the book business (there are lots of alternative technologies available to Yahoo!), but it will enable Amazon to do the same thing to electronic vendors in other categories.

Obviously, the seller can ultimately stop this game, if only by refusing to operate a Web site. But herein lies the second and more fundamental issue: *it is not obvious that it is in any one seller's interests to do so.* The most rigorously customer-affiliated navigator with the broadest reach is still a source of incremental business to a seller. Unless the selling business is highly concentrated, it is unlikely that the navigator's ability to achieve critical mass will depend on the availability of data from any one source. Therefore, while it is undoubtedly in the interests of all sellers *collectively*, it is not in the interests of any one seller *individually* to deny its own data to the navigator. But if everyone reasons that way, the navigator will achieve critical mass.[3]

The point is by no means merely theoretical. Consider the difficulties that the banking industry has experienced in combating the threat from Intuit, Microsoft, and other consumer-affiliated navigators. Many banks initially refused to support these "value-added browsers" for their customers, because they disliked their high reach and lack of seller affiliation. They pushed their own proprietary products instead. Industry groups solemnly agreed on collective strategies to fend off the threat. However, some banks saw supporting these new navigators as a competitive advantage in acquiring customers *from other banks*. For each bank deciding to do this, the gain in its *own* competitive advantage outweighed the slightly increased risk to the industry from giving those browsers a bit more critical mass. But as banks switch, the credibility, value added, and bargaining power of Intuit and Microsoft increase. Which makes it more logical for *other* banks to switch. The attempt to deny critical mass to consumer-affiliated navigators in banking is destined to fail for the same reasons cartels in general fail.

Frequently Asked Questions

1. **Is the shift to buyer affiliation a one-way move, or is this just a swing of the pendulum?**

    The explosion in reach is permanent, so the implied shift in affiliation is also permanent. Nonetheless, a lot of energy will be devoted by sellers to trying to preserve the affiliation of navigators, and some of it will succeed. Recognizing the permanence of the explosion of reach is essential to long-term competitive survival.

2. **Why don't navigators in cyberspace simply form tied vertical relations with suppliers, much the same way as their equivalents do in the physical world?**

   Because they don't have to and they don't want to. They don't have to because they can reach all suppliers, far more than in the physical world. They don't want to because of the competition from other navigators, which is much more intense and unstable than the equivalent in the physical world. A salesman has every reason to work for a supplier. Yahoo! has every reason not to.

3. **Can I charge for high-quality navigation?**

   Possibly, eventually. But not while others, rationally or not, are giving it away. Don't let uncertainty about charging stop you from offering high-quality navigation. The stock market has already decided that reach is worth more than current profits. Soon, the stock market will come to the same conclusion about richness.

While it is difficult for sellers to stop a navigator once it has passed the point of critical mass, it can also prove supremely difficult for the navigator to get to that inflection point. Amazon.com, tapping into a ready-made database, is the exception, not the rule. Jump-starting a network-based product or service is generally a huge challenge. Many seller-based navigators will survive for a long time, not because of clever defensive strategies, but because no consumer-affiliated navigator has the will and resources to mount a successful attack.

Greater Affiliation with Customers. The fourth line of defense is to embrace customer affiliation and try to become an advantaged navigator. Mimic, indeed exceed, the consumer orientation of the independent navigator. Offer a navigation service that solves problems instead of merely pushing product. Add in objective data and decision-support software about content unrelated to one's own business. Provide objective and comprehensive information about products and services in the consumer's search domain that one does *not* sell, commoditizing the businesses of others to protect one's own. Perhaps provide comprehensive but not necessarily comparable data on one's own products and those of direct competitors, and slightly bias the presentation through the ordering of alternatives and the occasional emphasis or omission. Possibly ally with noncompeting sellers in other industries that might have the same logic for partnering to support the chosen search domain. Conceal from the consumer the navigator service's supplier affiliation. All of these options (or combinations of them) are different forms of the same strategy. They involve giving up some measure of self-affiliation (relative to a captive navigator) in return for greater collective reach and closer consumer affiliation. The theory is that such a navigator may not be ideal for the seller, but is preferable to the independent alternative, and might suffice to deny to the latter critical mass.

It might work. It worked for American Airlines' SABRE system, where American was able to bias presentation of a comprehensive flight listing by giving its own offering slightly more richness and greater prominence.[4] But there are two problems. The first is that the navigator product is likely to be inferior (from the customer's point of view) to that provided by an independent third party. People are not that impressed by sellers announcing that they are being "objective." Even if they *are* objective, people will often refuse to believe them. Moreover, the symmetry and transparency of information flows, together with the obvious motivations of an independent navigator, will ensure that any self-serving injections of navigational bias will be loudly and widely noted. The hope has to be that some combination of timing, preemption, and alliance building can overcome limitations in reach and customer affiliation. In the airline customer reservations system (CRS) business, the staggering complexity of the data-processing requirements proved a lasting barrier to new entrants. But in many Web-based navigation businesses, the technical barriers are small. Therefore, one has to worry about the long-term defensibility of a "weakly biased navigator."

The second problem is a consequence of success. Suppose a TV manufacturer creates a "home theater" navigator that provides comprehensive and objective information about how to choose video and audio components (and, almost invisibly, presents its own products and technology in a favorably biased light). Suppose this navigator becomes popular. How, fearing commoditization, will the manufacturers of sound-processing systems or loudspeakers respond? With a parallel strategy, obviously. That might quickly lead to a half-dozen "home theater" Web sites, each offered by a coalition of rival sellers, each offering lots of consumer affiliation and comprehensive objectivity except for a *small* area in which the owners have a vested interest. But if such sites are all equally good, then the odds are five-out-of-six that a customer selecting one of these navigators to buy a TV set will *not* choose the TV manufacturer's. For the TV manufacturer (and by the same logic, for all other sellers), commoditization is avoided *only one-sixth of the time*. This implies a bit of a paradox: the consumer may *always* be guided by a seller-affiliated navigator, but it does not follow that the navigator will act to protect the interests of the particular seller whose product the consumer actually buys. Acting to protect their own individual businesses from commoditization, sellers happily commoditize each others'.

And fundamentally, of course, the reason why this happens in the virtual world, but not in the physical, is that the consumer's preferred virtual search domain does not correspond to any physical industry.

Co-option of the Navigator. The fifth line of defense is to do a deal with the navigator. Advertise on the navigator's Web site. Pay the navigator for each referral. Provide the navigator with some consideration in return for favorable navigational assistance. This cannot be done covertly (information about such arrangements will immediately become public), but it need not be highly visible. If the navigator business is still in an intense battle for critical mass, this may meet limited receptivity because the navigator thereby compromises its own competitiveness, and some navigators accepting such deals have been forced by consumer indignation to relinquish them. But if the navigator has already achieved a dominant position in some search domain, it may be quite open to the idea of an additional revenue stream. It is probable that many navigators (especially those with apparently captive audiences) will do profitable deals with sellers to give them exclusive or preferred positioning.

The obvious caution is that this goes against the long-term tide of increasing richness and reach, which separates the navigator business from the supplier business, and favors those navigators with the highest supplier reach and the richest customer knowledge. Every time an incumbent navigator makes a move in the reverse direction, a space is opened up for an insurgent navigator. And in the fluid world of information economics, there is no such thing as a locked-in position. Therefore either insurgent navigators chip away at the incumbent's position, or the incumbent is forced—eventually—to modulate the strategy. Meanwhile, however, the consumer tilt is forestalled.[5]

Deconstruction of the Seller's Business. The most extreme strategic response to these dilemmas is aggressive deconstruction of one's own value chain. Split the navigational function from the product supply function and let them operate as separate businesses. If the navigator then guides customers to competitor products and services, so be it. The customer relationship may matter more than the incremental product margin, at least in the long term. If the supplier business deteriorates, exit from it. Survive as a fully customer-affiliated navigator. Instead of treating navigation as a marketing function for a supplier business, think of products as a sourcing strategy for a navigator business. This may sound extreme, but some of the smartest and most aggressive commercial banks, institutions with hundreds of billions in assets, see this as their long-term strategy.

Escalation of Richness. The last, and probably most potent, line of defense is to forestall reach by escalating richness. This deserves a chapter of its own.

SOUND BITS

- Reach constraints make many navigators specific to sellers, and therefore they affiliate with sellers. Blow up the reach constraint, and those navigators tilt their affiliation toward buyers.

- The agency shift will force all players to tilt their own navigational offerings toward closer affiliation with the consumer and greater reach.

- The surprising thing is not that navigators will compete on the basis of consumer affiliation in the future; the surprising thing is that they did not do so in the past.

- The navigator business may be worth more than the supplier business; it is not obvious that the competitiveness of the former should be compromised for the benefit of the latter.

8

COMPETING ON RICHNESS

W<small>E HAVE DESCRIBED HOW</small> reach and affiliation can undermine the established structures of business and drain away much of their competitive advantage. We also have identified some counterstrategies for product suppliers and retailers. But by far, the most powerful way for incumbents and insurgents to compete, given deconstruction, is to use richness to deepen customer relationships and to build brand equity.[1]

Deconstruction is the corollary of the blowup of the richness/reach trade-off. As this trade-off shifts outward, it is almost inevitable that reach will go up, with all of the consequences that we have described in previous chapters. But it is equally possible and likely that sellers and navigators will exploit new technologies to offer greater richness. And, since the trade-off is displaced, not abolished, *the greater the increase in richness, the lesser will be the increase in reach*. The strategic priority, as illustrated in Figure 8-1, becomes to tilt "north" rather than "east." East is the direction of commoditization,

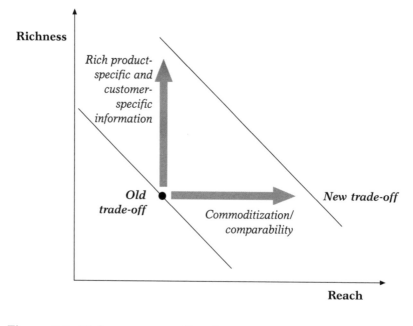

Figure 8-1: Richness versus Reach

disintermediation, and direct comparability. North is the direction of using information as a new glue to bond sellers and consumers into a stronger relationship.

Product suppliers can use richness to create value from a direct relationship with the consumer: not the pseudo-value of much current marketing communication, but real value based on a rich and voluntary exchange of information. If their product and brand lend themselves, they can build a rich multimedia channel for direct communication, and can thereby strengthen their position versus both established retailers and the new navigators who are crowding into the same space.

Retailers, both traditional and electronic, can and must try to do the same thing. Their wider product reach and closer consumer affiliation give them advantages versus the supplier, but they lack the supplier's deep product-related credibility, the ability to create a product-centered environment. The critical question becomes whether the richness that can usefully be added (usefully from the *consumer's* point of view, of course) maps better onto the supplier's narrow domain or the wider domain commanded by the retailer. This will vary from one category to another.

Richness Strategies

Information in a marketing context can be rich in two possible senses: it can be rich about the consumer, or it can be rich about the product. Rich consumer information is variously described as database marketing, data mining, or mass customization. Our term is *segment-of-one* since that comes nearest to capturing the essence of the strategy: using customer-specific information to execute customer-specific marketing. Rich product information encompasses all the obvious categories of technical facts, product background, and troubleshooting advice, plus everything that relates to branding.

Segment-of-one and brand information both operate as *shortcuts* through the consumer's hierarchical search process. Hierarchical searching is laborious and incomplete. The segment-of-one marketer identifies that the consumer needs, or is predisposed to, some particular configuration of product or services, and offers precisely that configuration to the prospective buyer, unprompted. The customization may not be quite as good as what the consumer would choose if she went through the full hierarchical search routine herself, but it is *good enough*. She takes the proffered "shortcut" through her decision hierarchy and buys the product.

Banks track birthdays and payroll credits to identify when their customers appear to have retired: they then offer financial planning services. Catalog companies buy, sell, and swap lists of customers with a known propensity to buy cookware or collectibles. Airlines and hotels customize discount offers based on the frequency and patterns of usage. Book clubs tailor their offers to the known or conjectured reading habits of each member. American Express—with one of the most comprehensive databases on the spending patterns of higher-income families—has mined that data to market some unlikely products: it is the largest vendor of clocks in the United States.

Brands similarly function as shortcuts through hierarchical choice. A brand is rich information on a product, associated service, and other attributes (whether real or perceived) in the mind of the consumer. The information comes from advertising, reputation, and, above all, prior experience. It is neither comprehensive nor necessarily objective, but it makes product choice *easy*. Brand knowledge enables the consumer to short-circuit the overly laborious and largely impossible task of trying to make choices systematically. Brand affiliation is remarkably stable: of the twenty-five top-selling consumer goods brands in 1960, sixteen of them are still among the top twenty-five today.[2]

Whether it is customer-specific or product-specific, sellers use rich information to lock in customer relationships and to lubricate the channels and habits of consumer choice in their own favor. Rich information offsets deconstruction.

The Impact of Exploding Reach

The explosion of reach affects the power of rich information strategies in two quite opposing ways. On the one hand, if reach increases *without an equivalent increase in navigability*, segment-of-one and branding become more powerful. As we argued in chapter 6, infinite choice, by itself, leads to nothing but infinite confusion. Faced with a bewildering array of choice, the consumer becomes more willing to rely on customized offers from sellers and more likely to rely on brand information from those few sellers able to rise above the clutter of competing claims. Much depends on the coherence and credibility of those claims: in some businesses, the seller's finely discriminated and elaborately customized offerings are the consumer's junk mail; in others (such as banking), intensive advertising campaigns have done little to fix a compelling brand image in the consumer's mind. But, in general, targeted marketing and consistent product messages have exhibited real staying power that will be *strengthened* by the proliferation of an unnavigable array of clamorous alternatives.

But conversely, if reach increases *in the context of structure and standards*, on the basis of which the usual array of databases, search engines, and comparison software all flourish, then the value to the consumer of seller-provided richness goes down. Navigators lower the cost of search, increase its comprehensiveness, and align the search process more closely with the interests of the buyer. If universal search thus becomes more efficient than it was before, there is less laboriousness to short-circuit, and more value for the consumer to gain from being systematic. Therefore rich information from sellers becomes less valuable to the consumer. This weakens the appeal of both segment-of-one and brands.

In this situation it is unlikely that customers would make a conscious decision to *stop* accepting unsolicited offers or *stop* buying on brand. The shift is less direct. Information becomes better and more symmetrically distributed. Customers therefore encounter snippets of information, occasional facts, comments, and comparisons that lead them to question whether this customized offer or that branding proposition was quite as good as they once had thought. The hints, the doubts, and the ease of experimentation then cause them to try out a few alternatives.

Brand position is complicated by the fact that universal navigation creates its own brands. Search has to begin somewhere. That starting point, by definition, cannot *itself* be reached via search. The searcher, based on advertising, reputation, or prior experience, must simply know it. But this means that the starting point is itself a brand. Yahoo! is a brand (and a very powerful one if its stock market valuation is to be believed). Navigator brands compete with conventional product brands for attention within the consumer's mind. Microsoft CarPoint, with its ability to search out new car models by specification, is potentially a rival brand not just to Auto Trader, but also, in a sense, to Ford. And if the set of brands with high unprompted recall is small, if the mental real estate occupied by power brands is necessarily limited, navigator brands may actually *displace* product brands.

The question for all businesses is how it is possible to use consumer- and product-specific rich information to strengthen relationships, rise above the clutter, and forestall the deconstructive impact of navigators.

Consumer-Specific Information

The advent of new information technologies offers powerful ways to expand segment-of-one capabilities. Electronic communication supports the collection and mining of detailed customer information files at very low cost. Although the underlying communications protocols of the Net are anonymous, browser programs accommodate "cookies" that are placed inside the user's machine and then record and transmit back detailed information about the user's activities. In principle, every site and page visited, every piece of information entered, every twitch of the mouse, can be tracked, recorded, and relayed back to the host server. This data can be used to target messages and offers based on *behavioral* (not just demographic or attitudinal) information about the consumer. And the Net can obviously then be used to deliver targeted offers with zero cost for postage.

For example, 1-800-FLOWERS has migrated from the telephone to the Internet as its primary communications channel with customers. This has enabled a much richer set of customized offers at minimal incremental cost. The company maintains a customer information file containing anniversary and birthday information and a record of previous gift purchases to specific recipients. It can thus provide alerts that a particular gift-giving event is coming up, and suggest gifts suitable to that individual and to the customer's price point. These gifts are no longer confined to flowers: the business is evolving into an electronic concierge service.

CDNOW lets its customers set up a personalized interface, "My CDNOW," by soliciting information on their favorite recording artists. CDNOW tracks this information and relates it to the individual's actual music purchases. It then applies a statistical matching technology, created by Net Perceptions,[3] to identify the universe of similar-minded people and recommend music that this larger group has purchased, but that might be unknown to the individual being matched. This brings to the individual's attention choices that she is likely to enjoy and might otherwise never have found. Of course, the motivation is to sell recordings, but many customers love the service and have become loyal to CDNOW in consequence.

We described in chapter 5 how Dell uses configurators to provide a richer interface to the consumer wishing to buy a computer on-line. Dell presents detailed choices and instantaneously prices the implications of those choices. In addition, Dell has created fifteen hundred customized home pages for its best corporate customers, so they get direct access to corporate-specified configurations, negotiated discounts, and records of orders and payments.[4]

More sophisticated configurators go beyond feature preferences to *needs*. Whirlpool, for example, is building an interface that asks about family composition, laundering frequency, and space constraints; calculates the specifications of the right washing machine; and recommends the closest match from the Whirlpool line.

Almost all companies who have offered configurator-type navigators have found that people tend to select *more* features than they would otherwise. The low-key passivity of the interface and the sense of control that it gives to the customer seem to sell more effectively than the lubricious ministrations of a salesman.

These technologies illustrate different ways in which companies have added richness to their own navigational interfaces and created value by so doing. In each case, companies are finding ways to offset or partially offset the threat of reach and the problem of agency affiliation. CDNOW's strategy makes it less likely that the customer will use a Junglee-based metanavigator to find the cheapest retailer for a chosen compact disc. Consumers are more likely to go to Dell or Whirlpool to configure their products, despite the narrow product line limitation, because the richness of the interface offers more utility than the reach available from more generic searches.

Suppliers and retailers are creating value for themselves and for their customers by exploiting rich information. This leads to the question of whether such strategies are sustainable in the longer run.

The first and most obvious issue is consumer privacy. Is the customer willing to allow such rich, comprehensive, and perhaps intimate data about him to be shared with a commercial enterprise that is trying to sell something, and that might choose to resell the data? In the physical world, limitations of richness and reach, more perhaps than laws or ethical self-restraint, have served as the principal protector of individual privacy. But those limitations are fast disappearing. Many people today instruct their browser not to accept the cookies that track their on-line activities. Many would be shocked if they knew how much information is collected about them today, albeit for generally harmless purposes.

Direct marketers are clearly right in their assertion that there is a "positive sum" element to the exchange of data between consumers and suppliers or retailers: consumers get information on products and services they want, and sellers get a more efficient channel for marketing and promotion. The issue is the *nonzero* elements: the ability of consumers to preserve anonymity, to prevent the reselling of personal information, to avoid "spam," to protect themselves against false information, to avoid being outgunned and manipulated by sellers armed with the latest in discriminant analysis. Moreover, while sellers can place cookies in the computers of consumers, consumers cannot place cookies in the Web sites of sellers: they cannot know what financial arrangements underlie the information and recommendations that are presented to them. Standards embedded in browsers (such as P3P: the Platform for Privacy Preferences) are one kind of solution. Standards voluntarily adopted by sellers and validated by certificate and audits (as operated by Trust-e) are another. Legislation, such as the European Data Protection Directive, is a third.

Absent regulation, perhaps the most likely evolution will be the promulgation of competing privacy codes, each with some kind of independent authority granting certificates of compliance. Electronic retailers and navigators will then be able to assert with credibility their conformity to a standard that the consumer can at least theoretically understand, and the consumer will be responsible for discriminating between one standard and another. But with the inevitability of abuse, the vulnerability of the unsophisticated, and the critical importance of consumer affiliation as a dimension of competitive advantage, any player pursuing a segment-of-one strategy will need to err on the side of caution and transparency in how information is used. Ethics aside, there is probably much more to gain in consumer affiliation from adhering to a tough voluntary standard than there is from exploiting rich information that consumers would not volunteer if asked. In competitive terms, privacy policy is destined to become the agency affiliation problem restated in a particularly acute form.

The second issue that gives pause is the possibility that the customer will backward integrate. In financial services, personal financial management software programs like Quicken or Microsoft Money include what are effectively configurators to enable consumers to compare and combine investment or loan options. To compare mortgages, customers don't have to rely on Citibank's mortgage calculator; they can use the one embedded in their own software, which provides the same objective comparison, the same navigational ease, the same rich information, but orders-of-magnitude greater reach and no confusion about agency affiliation.[5]

Just as it would be hard for a mortgage company to preserve its competitive position by providing a richly featured calculator for mortgage products, it is questionable whether, in the long run, Dell's configurator has a sustainable competitive advantage. Agent navigators could provide consumers with a rich interface for customizing their PC without restriction to one product line. Yahoo! or Amazon.com could use Junglee to do exactly that, and would have every motivation to give the navigational product away just for the advertising it would generate.

But how long does it take for this to happen? It may be that any *particular* rich capability will eventually be copied by the agent navigators, if only as Moore's Law makes it arbitrarily cheap and standards impose order on the domain. But by then, sellers will have moved on to something else. Part of the emerging competitive pattern is thus a continuous race between sellers and agent navigators: sellers creating reach-limiting richness and navigators then creating the standards that blow up that trade-off. Sellers succeed in using richness to forestall deconstruction to the extent that they can keep open a rich space not yet occupied by the navigators. Like the Red Queen in *Alice in Wonderland,* they must run hard in order to stand still.

There is a third possible issue. Segment-of-one strategies are predicated on building a uniquely rich customer information file: the advantaged competitor is the one with the richest file. But there are two parties to every transaction. The customer has the same information and could build—if she chose—the same file. In fact, she can build the least-cost, most comprehensive file about herself because she knows more about herself than anybody else does.[6] Privacy laws or conventions further increase the consumer's competitive advantage in the "customer information business." If that customer information file has value, *she can sell it.* The going rate would be the value of the information to marketers less the value of the information they already have. Thus the customer can arbitrage away the competitive value of a seller's elaborately constructed file. This does not happen in the physical world because it is actually very hard for consumers to track their own transactions systematically. It would be easy in the world of electronic commerce: third parties could *pay* consumers in cash or kind to install software to track and report on their behavior. The first thing such software would do is disable everybody else's cookies.[7]

This illustrates the infinite regress of deconstruction: *any strategy is vulnerable to an attack focused on unbundling its key source of informational competitive advantage.* In this case, the core asset of the segment-of-one strategy, the customer information file, provides the greatest competitive opportunity, not for the seller, but for the consumer. More generally, *any* consumer information–centered marketing strategy can theoretically be topped by a navigation strategy centered on the same information but with greater reach and better customer affiliation. The consumer has the greatest incentive to initiate or sponsor such a strategy. And some very smart people will try to make it happen.

The likelihood of consumers selling their own information files broadly is actually quite low, mainly because the degree of required critical mass is so high; before any real value is created, a comprehensive and uniform swath of consumer-specific information needs to be gathered and formatted for a large number of consumers. Moreover, the two sources of information—the buy side and the sell side of each transaction—would then become competing alternatives in a context where they are perfect substitutes for each other and have negligible marginal cost. This is a recipe for a permanently unprofitable business, which may suffice to deter serious players from pushing for critical mass that is uncertain anyway. Unlike so many other information business opportunities, this can never become a monopoly. Perhaps the biggest motive for consumers taking control of their own information would come from a breakdown of real and perceived respect for privacy. Paranoia, more than the economics of backward integration, could drive consumers to deprive sellers of all that rich information.

Each of these issues—privacy, backward integration by the customer, and deconstruction of the customer information file—poses limitations on the power of customer-specific information when the richness/reach trade-off significantly shifts. However, these do not invalidate the strategy: they simply delimit the range within which such strategies can flourish. By scrupulously respecting privacy concerns (which is a real, severe, and necessary limitation on the scope of the strategy), and by focusing and continually refocusing on rich information where agents have not yet created standards, both product suppliers and retailers have a powerful weapon in forestalling the deconstructive impact of reach.

Product-Specific Information

Many suppliers are exploiting product-specific information to enhance the utility of their current products and build richness that forestalls reach. In the music industry, for example, publishers are beginning to provide performer biographies, recording history, lyrics, chat rooms, and discographies, all as stand-alone Web sites, as rich information feeds to electronic retailers, and even directly to the consumer through enhanced CDs that go on-line when they are played on a computer. Part of their aim is to cross-sell from their catalog of past publications. Part is to build a cult following for the performer. Part is to provide to the whole electronic retailing industry the marketing capabilities that might otherwise be accessible only to Tower Records or to Amazon, and thereby to discourage retailer concentration and the attendant shift in bargaining power. This rich information strategy suffers limitations of reach: consumers often do not know where to go to access it. It has limitations in affiliation: producer-sponsored sites are generally not a credible source of picks and pans, or for the funky, anti-establishment rumor mill that endows performers' lives with such mythic significance. But as a low-cost means of enriching the music experience and maintaining a channel of communication around the retailers, the strategy is potentially quite powerful.[8]

Despite its disadvantages in reach and affiliation, rich navigational information from the product supplier can often be advantaged over that provided by a retailer or navigator. When the product is continuously evolving and the supplier provides state-of-the-art information about the latest breakthroughs, that can be of greater interest and utility to consumers than the comprehensive but dated offerings of a retailer or agency navigator. Manufacturers of digital cameras or cellular phones have an entirely legitimate advantage over a navigator in providing customers with information about the capabilities of these new and rapidly changing products. Because of the rate of change, the navigator is never able to establish an up-to-date standard to support comparability and exploit its advantage in reach.

The continuous change need not be technological. In highly price-sensitive product categories, such as long-distance telephone services and some financial service products, companies compete by continually changing their offerings just to minimize comparability. In these instances, while customers (and retailers) may dislike this behavior, they can be forced to use information provided directly by sellers because navigators cannot stay up-to-date. But navigators will try, and it becomes a cat-and-mouse game. In airline reservations, the cost of the product and the value of reach are high enough to warrant enormous efforts by the customer reservation system navigators (such as SABRE) to keep up with the complexities continually added by the airlines.

Supplier navigation can work where innovation is more cosmetic than real. Products like stereo components, cars, even kitchen knives, boast features that people *want* to believe in. The impressive if inscrutable technical claims presented in stereo literature—describing *"Uni-Q Technology* with its exceptional capacity to unify *co-planar* and *co-axial* directivity factors in the critical *crossover* region"[9]—may or may not withstand the objective scrutiny of engineering bench tests. But many an audiophile would rather read and believe such material (and brag about it to his friends) than confront a cold review in *Consumer Reports* suggesting that those $3,000 loudspeakers sound no better than a $300 pair available at Circuit City. "Affiliation," in this context, becomes a deeply ambiguous concept: it is not clear that *Consumer Reports* is doing the consumer a favor. Product literature, in a sense, becomes part of the product.

The product supplier can also be advantaged in sheer credibility. When a drug company asserts in advertising that a product offers certain benefits, it exposes itself to criticism, regulatory review, even lawsuits, if that proves not to be the case. The consumer knows this, and may, therefore, attach more credence to the assertion when it is made visibly and unambiguously by a large corporation (despite its obvious vested interest) than when the same assertion is made by some fly-by-night navigator whose only distinction is "objectivity." If the navigator is the family physician, however, it is not so obvious that the same logic applies.

Rich product information is thus a powerful but uncertain weapon for the product supplier. Wherever evangelism, enthusiasm, and a rich connotative context are welcomed by the consumer as product enhancing, richness strategies can be very effective. Wherever cool detachment, objectivity, and comprehensiveness matter more, such efforts may prove counterproductive.

Brands

Many of these same principles apply to brands, since a brand is nothing but rich, product-specific information acquired, retained, and believed by the consumer independent of any particular act of consumption. Shifts in the richness/reach trade-off have opposite effects on "brands as belief" and "brands as experience."

A brand as belief is knowledge that the seller communicates to the buyer about a product that can be paraphrased as a set of propositions about the product. A brand as experience is a set of rich communications from the seller to the buyer that *cannot* be paraphrased: feelings, associations, memories.[10] "Sony" is a brand as belief. Its brand proposition can be paraphrased as a set of product attributions: superior technology, higher manufacturing quality, miniaturization, and a modest but warranted price premium. Each of these things is a *belief* about Sony products; perhaps true, perhaps not. "Coca-Cola" is a brand as experience. The Coca-Cola brand cannot be paraphrased as a set of propositions *about* Coca-Cola. The brand *is* the taste, the curvy bottle, the logo, and the set of consistent emotional and visual connotations that the drink carries by merit of a century of advertising. It is simply an experience.

This is not a distinction of kind: all brands fall along a spectrum from belief to experience and contain elements of both.[11] Many product categories span a range. Some car brands are defined primarily in terms of belief, a set of propositions about reliability, efficiency, and features. Other brands are more strongly characterized by image, styling, and creating a sense that by owning the car, customers are making a statement about themselves. Toyota Corolla and Jaguar XK8 are very different branding propositions.

Rich information channels have very different impacts on branding belief and on branding experience. To the extent that a brand is a matter of belief, the brand message is fundamentally a *navigator* message. Buy this product and you will get the following attributes or features. Buy a Sony and you get better technology, lighter weight, and higher manufacturing quality. These are messages that an objective navigator could provide. *Therefore, the brand as belief competes with the navigator.* If a credible navigator repeatedly demonstrated that specific Sony products were not, in fact, better technology, lighter weight, and so forth, that would undermine the brand. It would be a contest of credibility between two means of navigation.

Indeed, even if the navigator validated Sony's claims every time, if people came to respect Sony products *because* of the navigator's endorsement, then the brand would become redundant. Brand as belief is no more than a generalization in people's minds about the features and performance of someone's products. Navigators reduce the need for such generalizations even when they continue to validate the specific claims being made. Thus precisely to the extent that the product is amenable to independent navigation, brand as belief is vulnerable too.

Brand as experience, however, is a different story. Barbie is a fantasy world for young girls and a collectible for adults. Mattel devotes enormous resources to creating and preserving the consistency with which that fantasy world is presented. Barbie is a brand as experience that will be *magnified* by richer channels of communication. When Mattel can reach young girls in a broadband, interactive, customized environment (as will be commonplace in a few years), it can enrich the Barbie fantasy world with dress up, storytelling, and conversations. This enhances the brand, but it also enhances the product and the experience of owning it. Indeed the brand, the product, and the experience are really one and the same thing.

Today, category killer retailers such as ToysRUs.com stand squarely between toy manufacturers and consumers. Mattel's ability to deliver the Barbie experience is constrained not just by the static nature of merchandising displays, but by shelf space and the unwillingness of the retailer to favor one toy company over another. The value of any richness created through the retail channel is taxed, if not expropriated, by the retailer. Direct, broadband presentation of the Barbie experience will enable the company to circumvent the retailer and create a brand as experience far more compelling than that in the physical store. Power shifts back to the supplier.

An electronic retailer, such as eToys or ToysRUs.com online, might respond by creating an interactive fantasy world featuring characters drawn from *multiple* vendors, closer perhaps to the way a girl actually plays with her toys.[12] Reach against richness. They might ally with educational broadcasters to create a more "uplifting" site, better calculated to win parental approval: affiliation against richness. *If* mixing up dolls or adding doses of political correctness is how young girls want to imagine the experience, those would be advantaged strategies. But probably not. Really strong brands as experience have a narrative force that transcends tinkering. Richness defeats reach.

Some brands as experience are single purchases rather than repeat buys like Barbie. Movies, for example, are brands with a limited theatrical shelf life. They are brands as experi-

The New Competitive Space

The new economics of information allows players to compete on *reach, affiliation,* and *richness.* Because of the blowup of the richness/reach trade–off, these become (really for the first time) free and independent dimensions for competitive positioning.

- **Product suppliers** can exploit reach to circumvent the retailer. But their long-term advantage is most fundamentally in richness, especially richness that is specific to their product. They need also to neutralize any disadvantage they may have in terms of customer affiliation.

- **Electronic retailers** are advantaged against traditional competitors in reach and potentially in consumer-specific information.

- **Agent navigators** can trump even the electronic retailers in reach and in affiliation, but must work hard to match the others in richness.

- **Traditional retailers** can go electronic and use their established brand and scale to beat the new electronic retailers at their own game. The only catch is that the traditional retailers need to attack their current business model.

- **Vertically integrated suppliers and retailers** are on all sides of these tensions, which is good and bad. It is good because they can make choices on how to compete. It is bad because they will often refuse to make those choices and will therefore get deconstructed by focused competitors.

ence created in part by intermixing another kind of brand, called film stars. Customers navigate to movies via film reviews and by watching advertisements and trailers. In contrast to a *Consumer Reports* review of toaster ovens, the film reviewer can proffer only an opinion: by definition, there is no objective basis for recommending a brand as experience. The independence of the film reviewer is worth something, but less when it is a matter of opinion than when it is a matter of fact. With the value of third-party navigation limited, trailers—mini-experiences of the brand—become powerful means of building brand awareness and enthusiasm. The ability to e-mail trailers to every desktop will, therefore, enhance the direct, experiential marketing of movies and diminish the role of the navigator. But then the logic of clutter reasserts itself. As every studio pushes this new promotional medium, the cacophony of competing brands will rise. The absence of standards, the absence of any basis of objective comparison, will make this explosion of reach unnavigable. The winners, as in any context of unordered choice, will be the brands strong enough to rise above the clutter. The tendency for the movie industry to be dominated by a small number of blockbusters will therefore be accentuated. Richness triumphs.

SOUND BITS

- Adding richness is the most powerful way to forestall deconstruction.

- Privacy is the Achilles' heel of the information economy: the long-term winners will be players who make a firm, public, and unambiguous commitment to a strong set of privacy standards and stick to them. Not only is that the right thing to do, it is also the competitively advantaged strategy.

- Remember that the consumer is your competitor: what are you doing for him that he cannot do for himself?

- The value of sellers' richness goes *up* as reach increases, since that is how they can grab attention and rise above the clutter; the value of sellers' richness goes *down* as navigators' richness catches up.

9

Deconstructing
Supply Chains

THE PREVIOUS THREE CHAPTERS discussed the deconstruction of a particular supply chain: the one linking consumers, retailers, and product suppliers. All the conclusions we have reached apply equally to *industrial* supply chains: those involving component manufacturers, service providers, OEMs, and distributors. The technologies are the same; the logic is the same; the opportunities and threats are basically the same.

The fact that these businesses are often about things, not information, is true but quite irrelevant: in an industrial context as much as a retail one, information is the glue that cements vertical linkages together and defines a large portion of competitive advantage. Deconstruction can emerge wherever reach is traded off for richness.

The players in industrial supply chains are obviously more hard-nosed and sophisticated than consumers; the transaction sizes are much larger; the value of reach is greater; affiliation is more likely to be defined contractually;

richness requirements are more complex and stringent. A lot of reach, in the sense of simple connectivity, is already installed and has been exploited by big corporations for years in the form of dedicated networks such as electronic data interchange (EDI). This connectivity is being transformed operationally as these expensive, proprietary systems are being replaced by "extranets"[1] that are built on the same open and universal TCP/IP protocols as the Internet. But the key challenge is not technical, it is *strategic*: building on connectivity to establish *standards*.

Standards in an industrial context are much more valuable, but also much harder to create and drive to critical mass. Therefore, the deconstruction of industrial supply chains depends much more acutely on the high-stakes, high-risk, and highly problematic game of building such standards. This inserts a degree of *radical uncertainty* into the industrial context. It means that the winners will be bold strategists who build the right coalitions and commit a sufficient level of resources to standards-based strategies that happen to succeed. Like crystals dropped into a solution, their impact when successful will be to precipitate a realignment of whole industries. And realignments *across* industries as well: there is absolutely no reason why the economics of information should compartmentalize itself within a straitjacket defined by the economics of things.

The Spectrum of Scale

The trade-off between richness and reach is really three-way: richness versus reach versus *cost*. Spend enough money, even with old technologies, and most levels of richness and reach become somehow attainable. And such expenditures become worth the cost when the parties to the transaction, and its size and frequency, become large enough. This defines a *spectrum of scale* within the universe of supply chain relations. The logic of deconstruction operates differently at various points along it.

- When big corporations deal with each other on big-ticket information-intensive transactions, they have typically already installed EDI systems. Wall Street trading houses, and automotive manufacturers with their Tier One suppliers, already operate sophisticated and dedicated networks. These may be inflexible and based on old mainframe technologies, but *they already have the degree of richness and reach they want*. The impact of new technologies is therefore *operational* rather than strategic: they allow for greater functionality and lower operating costs.

- At a somewhat smaller size of corporation and transaction (many retailer-supplier contexts, for instance), the current information infrastructure sacrifices reach: companies lock in supplier-customer relationships in order to justify the high cost of rich EDI communication. Wal-Mart's relation with many of its mid-sized suppliers falls into this category. The impact of new technologies is therefore to allow the substitution of open for proprietary communication platforms: common standards allow for an expansion of reach and a loosening of vertical ties.

- For less sophisticated companies and even for large corporations, when transactions are small and peripheral to the main line of business (buying stationery as opposed to buying components), the odds are that no special communications and transactions infrastructure has been put in place. Phone, fax, and personal

Rolodex suffice. Here the possibility of a rich, cheap, data- rather than voice-based infrastructure permits an explosion of reach and comparability, with negligible costs of searching and switching. It is here that the impact most resembles what we saw in the consumer arena.

- When small companies deal with each other, simply finding each other is a challenge, and reach constraints impose search costs and market inefficiencies. Market makers have a major opportunity to connect such companies together, allowing a degree of fluidity in transactions and collaboration traditionally possible only within the boundaries of the corporation.

The spectrum of scale defines a *sequence* in terms of which deconstruction is likely to have an impact on supply chains. Big corporations introduce new technologies as operational upgrades, lowering costs and raising the reliability and functionality of things they are doing already. Almost as a byproduct, these new technologies prove readily extensible to smaller transactions, to smaller companies in their dealing with the large, and eventually to smaller companies in their dealings with each other. Where the large corporations are uninterested or unable to play the catalyzing role, market makers then flourish. For smaller companies, this opens up new channels for marketing and sourcing, eliminating many of the informational barriers that have constrained their external relations. For everyone, it allows reach outside the established linear sequence of the supply chain, so that OEMs can communicate and collaborate effectively with their suppliers' suppliers or their distributors' distributors. And over time, dominant players or market makers introduce progressively more sophisticated information standards that support rising levels of richness. This enables separate enterprises to achieve a degree of close collaboration and coordination that had heretofore been possible only within the confines of hierarchical organization.

Deconstructing the Automotive Supply Chain

The Automotive Network Exchange, ANX, is the world's largest extranet, already involving over five thousand companies in the automotive supply chain worldwide. Sponsored initially by the Big Three Detroit OEMs, ANX will provide the industry with a nonproprietary, global communications network that is built on Internet technology. By using dedicated, high-performance routes and special protocols, the network guarantees fast connections and levels of reliability and security well beyond those available on the standard Internet or on most proprietary data networks. The network operator contracts with chosen Internet service providers to provide and maintain a high-performance physical network within the public Internet architecture, rather like leased lines from the phone company. On this physical infrastructure, ANX then operates as an open utility, just like the Internet, but with industrial levels of speed, reliability, and security. It supports communications across all participating companies, and also provides "virtual private networks" for its members, allowing employees within a company to communicate securely with one another.[2]

One auto industry executive compares ANX to "what the Telcos achieved fifty to seventy-five years ago with universal connectivity. You can pick up a telephone and are guaranteed a dial tone. ANX is the data tone for the auto industry."[3]

Over time, ANX will promulgate a series of standards for different kinds of transactions, which will then be mandated

by the major OEMs. It will quickly support videoconferenc-
ing and IP telephony. Production and logistics will become
closely coupled across the entire supply chain as all participants exchange the kind of scheduling detail that only large
players with common EDI systems can share today.[4] Auto-
mated supplier-bidding standards will enable contracts to be
announced and bid among companies who hardly know each
other. Teams will be able to share applications on ANX servers so that engineers from different companies around the
world can swap computer-aided design and engineering files
and see one another's changes in real time during meetings.

The most obvious and immediate impact of ANX will be
on costs. Currently, OEMs and their big, Tier One component suppliers use proprietary networks to communicate
with each other. These EDI networks are generally not
interoperable, and use incompatible and duplicative technology. Chrysler, for example, has thousands of lines to its Tier
One suppliers. "We are quite literally a phone company," one
executive at the company complained.[5] As these systems are
replaced with a single open network, communication costs
will plummet. Further down the supply chain, phone and
fax are the protocol of choice; here, ANX will not only cut
costs, but also speed up communication and eliminate errors.
Today a specification change announced in Detroit takes
about ninety days to be communicated along the entire supply chain, employing a corporate variant on the game "Chi-
nese Whispers." ANX will reduce that to a matter of
minutes. According to an industry estimate, if twenty thousand companies are eventually connected, the industry will
save around $1 billion a year from less costly information
processing and faster data transmission. That translates into
about $70 per car sold.[6]

Much more important, however, ANX will lower costs
indirectly by intensifying competition throughout the supply

chain. The new standards will make it easy for buyers to post supply requirements on electronic bulletin boards, manage a real-time bidding process, and maximize comparability and competition among their would-be suppliers. This is not an innovation for the largest companies, where such bidding practices are already the norm, but the impact of ANX will be to carry that sophistication to the Second and Third Tier companies in dealing with *their* suppliers. (Second and higher tier suppliers account for more than half of the value added in the automotive industry.) As in the consumer world, an explosion of buyer's reach lowers the value of "relationships" and intensifies competition on the basis of product-specific characteristics: quality, timeliness, and price (see Figure 9-1).

New intermediaries are operating on top of ANX to develop standards in specific businesses. CIMSOURCE, an effort supported by leading cutting tool suppliers in Germany, has developed a catalog of over 100,000 distinct cutting tool products, comprising the full product lines of over fourteen leading manufacturers. Currently, the database is available only on CD-ROM, but a Web-based application is being created. The database allows buyers to search for products based on specific parameters and compare product performance. CIMSOURCE also provides CAD images and application guidelines to explain the latest cutting technology. Tool manufacturers gain reach to a worldwide market; buyers gain reach to a comprehensive, navigable universe of product alternatives.[7] Although pricing is not currently available, still less on-line transactions, these are natural extensions of the service.

For many suppliers, such as the manufacturers of cutting tools, this means the intensification of what is already a very competitive marketplace. It forces them to consider a strategy of rigorously low product cost, associated, perhaps, with

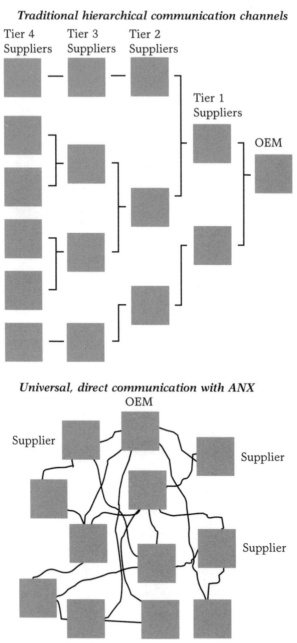

Source: Philip B. Evans and Thomas S. Wurster, "Strategy and the New Economics of Information," *Harvard Business Review,* September–October 1997, p. 75.

Figure 9-1: ANX: Universal, Direct Connectivity Undermines Traditional Hierarchy

a product line focused on long-run, standard items. Those selecting such a strategy would then rely on a low-cost market maker like CIMSOURCE to reach high-volume, price-sensitive customers. Conversely, a manufacturer might choose to concentrate on specialty products and custom solutions. This avoids the standards, bidding procedures, and pressure toward commoditization, but would still exploit ANX as a rich platform for counseling and problem solving with customers on the other side of the world.

Changing the Competitive Landscape

ANX will generate big opportunities for players with genuinely better mousetraps. A small Tier Four supplier with a design idea or a process innovation will be able to reach dozens of partners cheaply: it may even be able to influence the OEM with whom it normally has no dealings. ANX opens the possibility of leapfrogging the traditional supply chain hierarchy and enabling direct collaboration among players at noncontiguous levels.

ANX will also allow small suppliers to collaborate much more easily and effectively with each other. They will be able to share resources, design products together in real time, engage in simultaneous engineering, and even form "virtual companies" for joint bidding on major projects. OEMs welcome this. Part of their philosophy is to look to their suppliers for *systems*: integrated engineering solutions, rather than mere components manufactured to specification at least cost. Suppliers realize that they cannot compete by arrogating to themselves a monopoly on design and innovation. Therefore, fluid and self-organizing collaboration among suppliers—not just the top dozen where it happens already, but deep into the universe of small companies where so much innovation occurs nowadays—represents a fundamental managerial goal that ANX enables.[8]

This is a sea change in managerial thinking. The lower tiers of the automotive industry are traditionally associated with low-tech, cost-based subcomponent manufacture: stamping plants in Mexico and the like. Soon a Tier Four or Five supplier will be much more likely to be a high-technology company, say in Silicon Valley. OEMs need to understand what these small companies are doing, collaborate on new applications, and then drive the resulting innovations through all the intervening tiers of the manufacturing supply chain. ANX provides the beginnings of an infrastructure that allows the kind of rich, recombinant innovation that Silicon Valley is famous for, but enables it to flourish across barriers of geography, industry, and corporate culture.

ANX has so much momentum because the Big Three in Detroit are strongly committed to it. Because the U.S. automotive industry is so concentrated, these three firms can simply mandate standards in the assurance that their supplier industries will quickly conform. The U.S. government and a few large retailers could do the same (indeed the U.S. government did so in its original sponsoring of the Internet). But most industries are not dominated by a few strong players, so the cumulation of critical mass elsewhere is far less certain.

The Migration of Standards

ANX is not the only application of networks and standards. OASIS defines transmissions capacity transactions among electricity utilities. CPFR provides a basis for logistical and marketing coordination between retailers and their suppliers. GE Information Services is building a market making business for industrial products based on the categories of Thomas's Register. RosettaNet is an organization of twenty-nine companies, including Microsoft, CISCO, Sun, and Netscape, that is creating a master dictionary that "defines properties for products, partners, and business transactions."[9] Using a standard called the Partner Interface Process (PIP), the dictionary allows firms to define, search, and then request and respond to bids on any product that has dictionary-defined specifications (see Table 9-1).[10]

Table 9-1: Content Standards Initiatives Exist in Many Industries

Industry	Standard	Description
Nonindustry specific	RosettaNet	Master dictionary of properties for products, partners, and transactions
Financial services	Open Financial Exchange (OFX)	Financial data exchange between financial institutions, businesses, and consumers
Electric utilities	Open Access Same-time Information System (OASIS)	Transmission capacity transactions among electricity providers
Retail	Collaborative Planning, Forecasting, and Replenishment (CPFR)	Point-of-sale, inventory, marketing, and promotional data exchange between retailers and manufacturers
Health care	HL7/KONA	Electronic health record creation, exchange, and processing among providers and managed care organizations

Sources: OFX Web site (< www.ofx.net >); WebOASIS Web site (< www.weboasis.com >); "Trading Partners Unite—New Standards Take Guess Work out of Supply Chain Management," *Internet Week*, 23 February 1998; KONA Web site: (< www.mcis.duke.edu/standards/HL7/sigs/sgml/WhitePapers/KONA >); RosettaNet Web site (< www.rosettanet.org >).

Even when these innovations appear to be industry-specific, they are not. Standards migrate. The steel, rubber, glass, machine tool, hydraulics, plastics, and many other industries are all adopting ANX standards in their capacity as suppliers to the automotive industry. Once adopted, it becomes natural for them to use these standards in their dealings *with each other*, and to mandate those standards for companies over whom they in turn have influence. There are already signs that the basic architecture and some of the key applications of ANX are moving quite rapidly beyond the confines of the automotive industry. Once a standard achieves critical mass, the interconnectedness of *all* physically defined industries ensures that it will inexorably spread to fill the entire domain in which it is competitively advantaged.

ANX is a story. It contains the familiar themes of deconstruction: connectivity and standards, the explosion of richness and reach, self-organization substituting for hierarchy, and the economics of information spilling outside the traditional confines of the economics of things. It is a story that will eventually subsume the strategy of every company in the automotive industry and many beyond, and it is a story that is rapidly filling a global stage. We can tell it as a narrative, quite confidently even in prospect, because *the point of critical mass has been reached*, and the direction is therefore clear.

But what if there were no Big Three? What if the industry was two or three times larger and the biggest player one-tenth of the size? How would the logic of deconstruction affect a more fragmented, even more complex industry, like health care?

Deconstructing Health Care

Health care is the largest information business in the U.S. economy. As mentioned in chapter 2, one-third of its trillion-dollar cost is the cost of creating and processing information.[11]

As an information industry, health care is complex and inefficient. The industry is a web of fixed communication channels established between patient and physician, physician and hospital, physician and plan provider, plan provider and employer, primary care physician and specialist, physician and drug company. For each pair-wise relationship, there is a substantial cost of setup, and the information records that sustain the relationship are then kept in different and noncomparable ways by each player.[12]

This makes it difficult, expensive, and time-consuming for any participant to exercise the simplest forms of reach. The lack of standards and the portability of information make it very difficult for patients to get second opinions or to compare outcomes data for different institutions or procedures. It is hard for physicians to change hospital or plan affiliation or to scan the qualifications of specialists, and employers cannot effectively compare and switch among plan providers. Drug companies find it difficult and costly to track the safety and efficacy of their products in clinical practice.

Within this web of locked-in contractual relationships lie complex arrangements for the distribution of risk. In some arrangements, the risk is borne by the plan, in others by the patient, in others by the provider. This creates *agency* problems, since patients, providers, and employers acquire different interests as a function of who bears the risk. These agency problems and the substantial *asymmetries* of information among the various players lead to cumbersome systems for monitoring and control. Employers, through health plans, try to influence the behavior of patients and providers, often against their will or professional judgment.

Risk redistribution implies risk pooling and therefore cross-subsidies. The well subsidize the sick; different departments, procedures, illnesses, and institutions subsidize each other. While part of this is deliberate policy, reflecting the fact that health care is not a commodity to be bought and sold like soda, part reflects a deep inability to know just where costs are actually incurred. Hospitals and health plans function like department stores, with only the vaguest grip on how the economics of their separate activities add up to the economics of the whole.

The result is a system hated by everyone: bureaucratic, expensive, difficult to navigate, opaque, and riven by unadmitted conflicts of interest and intrusive controls. Richness within the physician-patient relationship, but precious little reach for either doctor or patient outside the fixed and prewired channels that constitute the informational structure of the industry.

A number of new and innovative players are trying to chip away at these problems by using electronic data capture, creating open and comparable information standards, and offering greater reach and navigation to patients, physicians, and employers.

- Several thousand Web sites and chat rooms have proliferated, devoted to health care topics that range from allergies to acute illnesses. Especially for low-grade and unusual illnesses (hepatitis C is a prominent example), these communities of interest have become an important source of mutual education for patients and for physicians.[13]

- *Consumer Reports* is publishing reader reviews comparing managed care plans. Data include degree of choice, doctor quality and availability, and waiting time for service. This information is available in the magazine and via a Web-based service.

- Decision Innovations, a company based in North Carolina, employs conjoint technology to help patients choose a managed care plan. A patient answers a series of questions regarding the relative importance of such issues as waiting time, cost, and risk. Relating that information to a database of plan characteristics, the company then recommends the plan that would best suit the individual's needs.[14]

- Access Health, an employer-paid service based in California, helps people select appropriate sources of treatment. When a patient has a problem, she first calls Access Health, which performs a quick diagnosis and directs her to an emergency room, a primary care physician, or some form of self-treatment. This simple triage has reduced unnecessary use of high-cost emergency rooms and thereby lowered the overall cost of treatment. Employers seem delighted: Access Health has a 95 percent retention rate.

- HealthPartners in Minneapolis has created a rudimentary rating and pricing system for helping consumers choose physicians and hospitals. The company publishes information on participating physicians' credentials, experience, hospital affiliation, and clinical outcomes as defined by the National Committee for Quality Assurance (NCQA). Physicians place themselves in a pricing tier: a standard rate covered by insurance, a 10 percent premium, or a 20 percent premium, both paid by the patient. Equipped with comparative data and pricing options, consumers are then free to make a more informed and market-based choice.

As a result of the availability of better information on outcomes, employers are beginning to use this information to question the choices made by managed care organizations. Better-informed patients are beginning (rightly or wrongly) to question their physicians' recommendations. Tertiary providers of specialist and acute care are starting to compete for primary care referrals on the basis of outcomes, and for plan sponsorship on the basis of cost-effectiveness.

Each of these developments represents the promulgation of a standard, the creation of navigational services, and support for connectivity and comparability, allowing participants variously to achieve greater richness and reach. But relative to the enormity of the informational rigidities in the industry, none comes close to critical mass: as yet there is no equivalent in health care to ANX.

The Patient Record

One crystallizing event for health care would be the promulgation of a standard for electronically maintaining and sharing patient records. Today, providers and managed care organizations have partial versions of each patient's record, each kept in its own format. Large portions of the record are handwritten, and parts of it are X-rays and other specialist information kept in analog form. For lack of a standard, physicians re-collect the same information; records can be transferred only by physical delivery; protocols and outcomes can be compared only through laborious and inaccurate human interpretation; and plans, drug companies, and researchers cannot measure outcomes systematically.

If there were a universal standard patient record, it could be stored on smart cards that patients carry, backed up to a server on-line.[15] Patients could e-mail their complete records to any provider and receive a consultation or diagnosis virtually: not a substitute for a personal examination of course (some kinds of richness/reach trade-off are inherent in medicine) but still of considerable utility. The cost of a second or third opinion, the cost of switching providers, and the cost of dealing with multiple providers for multiple conditions would all plummet.

On the basis of a standardized patient record, *outcomes*—by provider, by population group, or by treatment protocol—could be measured systematically across a large universe. Patients, and their primary care physicians, could use that information to choose the best provider of specialist treatment. Specialist tertiary providers of care for acute conditions could be subjected to rigorous scrutiny and therefore competition on quality. Insurers and employers could use outcomes information as a basis for setting more discriminating rules for treatment and approvals.

On the basis of a standardized patient record, physicians, researchers, and drug companies could track the longitudinal course of patients' chronic conditions, as opposed to the history of individual episodes that is captured today. They could use longitudinal information to measure the impact of early interventions on the lifetime history of the disease. Insurers knowing the lifetime economics of a disease could encourage providers to focus more, and even spend more, on early prevention: improving patient health and cutting lifetime costs simultaneously.

Standardizing patient information could be a boon for drug companies. Today drug companies conduct massive research programs to test the efficacy of different treatment protocols by using populations of volunteers as a basis for gathering standardized information. If standardized patient records existed and health care providers shared sanitized or aggregated data on patients and treatments, then drug companies would have a ready-made database, much larger than any test population they use today. They would be better able to evaluate and fine-tune the efficacy of different regimens, and could identify promising areas for future research.

Standardized patient records would even transform the logic of risk pooling. If patient records were comprehensive and uniform, actuaries could exploit the size and uniformity of the database to develop fine-tuned discriminations in the cost of health care for different people, and even for different kinds of illness. Insurers could then use that knowledge to target the subsidizing, and avoid the subsidized, portions of the market. As with the commercial property insurance business, people could purchase different kinds of insurance for different tiers of risk, possibly for different types of illness. They could choose to self-insure for a wide range of liability that is covered under health plans today. Insurance for people with strong health records would become cheap, and that for people with poor health records would become expensive. If carried far enough, the insurability of whole sections of the population could collapse.

This kind of logic could ultimately drive employers out of the business of financing health care. When employees no longer constitute a meaningful risk pool, when insurance choices proliferate, when frictionless portability across plans and providers becomes the norm, employers may simply provide employees with a cash benefit and leave it to the employees to buy health care on whatever basis they choose. Many employees might decide to buy large proportions of their health care over the counter—without the intermediation of any kind of insurer. The average middle-class family might buy insurance to protect themselves against catastrophic illnesses but forgo insurance for treatment of day-to-day complaints. The evolution would be much like that of pensions: today employers give their employees money through 401(k) plans, and employees make their own decisions on how to invest it.

Our point is not that any of this is destined to happen, still less that it is necessarily desirable. Our point is simply that connectivity and standards—critically, a uniform patient record—would have devastating implications for the deconstruction of the vertical information bonds and locked-in relationships that bind players in the health care industries together. *If* such standards were developed, *if* they reached critical mass, then for better or for worse, reach would explode, established relationships would fall apart, cross-subsidies would become untenable, and focused competitors would maximize profits by picking off the richest slivers of the market. Over wide swaths of the industry, the direct purchase of medical services would substitute for insurance: the social and moral fabric of risk sharing and strong helping weak (tenuous as it is even today) would fall apart.[16]

None of this is to deny the centrality of the relationship between patient and physician, or the intuitive, humanistic side of medicine. Nor is it to preclude or argue against governmental intervention to protect the interests of the economically disadvantaged. Nor is it to downplay the importance of entirely legitimate concerns over the privacy of medical records. Our point is simply that key information standards, if driven to critical mass, would precipitate a deconstruction of the information-bonded relations in the health care industry, just as they have already done in industries less complex and less fraught with moral and social ambiguities.

But will it happen? There is no obvious momentum, at least at the moment. Industry study groups are working on a master standard for clinical data called HL7, and some specific patient record formats have been proposed, notably KONA. Administrative standards have been proposed by the Health Insurance Portability and Accountability Act (HIPAA). Repeated efforts to establish such standards have foundered

Frequently Asked Questions

1. **When will all this happen in my industry?**

   That's like trying to predict an earthquake. We can see
   the pressures build, we can know (for certain industries)
   that enormous value would be released, we can know
   that the release requires some particular, identifiable
   standard to reach critical mass, and we know that such a
   standard could always be driven to critical mass in
   another industry and then migrate across. We can demonstrate (for some industries) that they are sitting on the
   business equivalent of a tectonic fault line. We can be
   reasonably sure that the earthquake is going to happen,
   because the pressure is simply too great. But it is impossible to say specifically *when*. Strategy has to live with
   that uncertainty.

2. **To what extent do the arguments in chapters 6–8
   apply to industrial companies?**

   They apply closely in the relations between small
   companies and large, which are essentially the same as
   the relations between consumers and corporations. For
   large companies in those relations, the issues of reach,
   the rise of navigators, affiliation, competing on customer-
   specific information, and competing on product brand
   are *exactly* the same.

   For small companies dealing with each other, the
   issues of reach and navigation are the same, but richness
   and brand are less likely to matter.

   For large companies dealing with other large companies, the key issue is the richness of organic collaboration, which can be carried to new levels of sophistication.

on disagreements among the experts on format and content. A major breakthrough may come from XML (eXtensible Markup Language) technology, which allows a database to describe itself. This would permit different institutions to continue to store patient information in their own ways, but the common XML language would permit seamless cross-reference and comparison.

In Europe, the national health services are likely to be the standard-sponsoring equivalent of ANX. In the United States, an alliance of health plans might exercise sufficient clout. Or perhaps the ANX of health care will be ANX: the auto industry spends more on health care than it does on steel, and might choose one day to focus its energies on rationalizing one of the biggest elements of its cost structure. Nobody really knows. The industry is ripe for some form of deconstruction, and the principles and consequences are clear for all to see. But the will, the vision, and the sheer economic power are yet to be exercised.

Deconstructed Supply Chains

The evolution of extranets, and of the content standards that then displace the richness/reach trade-off, will dramatically alter the bases of competitive advantage. They will diminish the value of established business relationships. Greater reach will allow buyers who want the best product to find suppliers who offer the best product—worldwide. Greater richness will allow companies that have complex and intractable problems to solve, or tasks to complete, to get help from others who can bring the needed skills and technologies—again, worldwide.

Outsourcing will flourish, because reach to the best product suppliers is greater, because specifications are easier to agree on, and because mutual dependency is minimized by the availability of alternatives.

Market making will also flourish, as companies who are themselves big purchasers discover that their own volume can jump-start a stand-alone business to bring buyers and sellers together. Such market making businesses (following the economics of information, not the economics of things) will quickly evolve beyond the confine of the parent's original purchasing mix. This will be a major route through which efficiencies achieved by the large quickly filter down to benefit the small.

Decentralized self-organization—the ability of employees to group together, break apart, and regroup across corporate boundaries—will flourish as small companies exploit richness and reach to collaborate with each other. As enterprises learn to do this, they will demonstrate the ability to complete complex projects that had previously been possible only through the hierarchical direction of the large corporation.

The ultimate challenge posed by deconstructing supply chains will be to the organization itself. If multiple, smaller organizations can self-organize and collaborate through a pattern of fluid alliances, this raises an interesting question as to why, precisely, the large hierarchical corporation is needed at all. Perhaps there is not much difference between self-empowering teams within the corporation and deconstructed supply chains among corporations. Perhaps, in fact, there is not much difference between what happens within the modern corporation and what happens across its boundaries. Perhaps the boundaries don't really matter.

We now turn to that final question.

SOUND BITS

- In an industrial context, connectivity is already achieved; standards are the more critical challenge.

- Strategy has to live with *radical uncertainty* governing the evolution of standards. The need and the value of standards are easy to identify; but whether and where they will emerge, and who will control them, may be impossible to predict.

- Extranets, standards, and market-making businesses start within industries, but they do not stay there. They follow the economics of information, not the economics of the things the industry manufactures.

- The explosion of richness and reach will change the bases of competitive advantage and intensify competition at all levels of the supply chain.

- Extranets encourage outsourcing. They simultaneously lower the transaction's cost, increase the benefits, and diminish the risks.

10

DECONSTRUCTING the ORGANIZATION

As WITH VALUE CHAINS and supply chains, business organization is deconstructed as the trade-off between richness and reach blows up. New organizational models become possible—models that afford much more richness *and* reach.

Shifts in the richness/reach trade-off (driven, as always, by connectivity and standards) have already enabled substantial deconstruction of investor relationships. Currently, deconstruction is beginning to reshape labor markets. Comprehensive deconstruction of employment and investment is starting to result in more fluid business environments, such as Silicon Valley, and this comprehensive form poses a fundamental challenge to the entire logic of the large corporation.

The Traditional Hierarchical Organization

It is easy to find fault with hierarchical organization—it can be slow, cumbersome, bureaucratic, and politicized. But it

remains the basic model of how economic activity is organized. And it will continue to be the dominant type of
organization in many sectors of the economy for years to
come.

The traditional organization is built on the severe constraints imposed by the trade-off between richness and
reach. Within the traditional organization, the economics of
information has always been determined at least in part by
the economics of the physical entities that the organization
has existed to manage. (That's the reason, for instance, that
offices have been located next door to factories.)

The resulting trade-off has made it difficult to move information around, and the organization has been structured to
accommodate that limitation. The hallmarks of a classic hierarchy—division of labor, accountability, discipline, predictabil-
ity—are all consequences of the trade-off between richness
and reach.

Because large numbers of employees cannot communicate richly and directly with one another, the traditional
organization has layers of middle managers switching information up and down and across the organization. The span
of control within the traditional organization chart—the fact
that no one can effectively manage more than a limited number of direct reports—can be thought of as a measure of the
reach constraints within which the organization operates.

The classic hierarchy therefore supports rich coordination
within a reach defined by common reporting relationships. It
is a vehicle for placing important decisions in the hands of a
single individual whose managerial span encompasses the
requisite resources, and for ensuring that his subordinates
are held precisely accountable for executing his will.

The problems of coordinating a hierarchy are reduced to
the extent that it is possible to break down the overall business into tasks that have *as little to do with each other as*

possible. Organizational units are defined to *minimize* the extent to which they need to collaborate with each other. Moreover, because of the high setup costs for information channels, they cannot be changed very frequently. Companies have to "hard-wire" their reporting structures and information systems and then live with their choices. Regardless of whether the hierarchical structure is defined by functions, markets, or geographies, it is a set of static information channels that reduce the amount of information that needs to be moved around to a manageable level. The problem of hierarchical organizational design is thus one of *partitioning* the managerial task into as discrete and independent a set of tasks as possible, and then building a *fixed* set of information channels that support that partition.

The severe trade-offs between richness and reach result in asymmetries of information. Senior executives have a more comprehensive grasp of the "big picture." Subordinates have more detailed knowledge of what is going on in their respective departments. This asymmetry necessitates complex structures to maintain control. Corporate staff, management information and reporting systems, and a philosophy of strict accountability are necessary to make sure that employees farther down in the organization are pursuing the interests of the corporation at large.

Asymmetries of information imply asymmetries of power: the political games we all recognize as revolving around monopolizing various kinds of knowledge. To minimize politicization, the traditional hierarchical organization emphasizes formality, discipline, and impersonality. Commitment to the company and to the integrity of its "system" is essential to its workings and legitimacy. *Fairness* is a key part of its value system, often at the expense of rewarding the highest performers with their economic worth (or, for that matter, penalizing the worst performers). People are promoted and paid differently within a set of constraints defined by what is deemed equitable.

Markets and Hierarchies

Traditional hierarchies support higher richness but lower reach; markets support higher reach but lower richness.*

Hierarchies encourage *collaboration*: people within an organization are able to work together without having to negotiate responsibilities and rewards in great detail beforehand, because it is their common employer who bears the risk. In markets, however, there is no third party to bear the upside and the downside, so every contingency in the collaboration has to be negotiated between the principals, or by their lawyers. However, by minimizing informational and moral interdependency and by concentrating risk and reward, markets make *initiative* easier and potentially much more rewarding. The choice between markets and traditional hierarchies is thus a trade-off between collaboration and initiative.

Hierarchies are amenable to leadership and to strategy. Markets, in general, are not. Hierarchies can exploit nonlinearities: they can make strategic moves that do not pay off initially, but may eventually with time and luck. However, markets adapt incrementally and without the political complexities of hierarchies. They evolve more like biological systems. Unless led by governments or a coalition of dominant players, they follow their noses: each evolutionary step that proves a success encourages the next.

However, as new organizations create market-like mechanisms internally and collaborative mechanisms externally, these distinctions break down. We are seeing the emergence ▼ of hybrids that achieve more richness *and* reach, a better trade-off between collaboration and initiative, and a better balance between strategy and adaptability.

*For the classic accounts of the relationship between hierarchies and markets, see Ronald Coase, *The Firm, the Market and the Law* (University of Chicago Press, 1990) and Oliver Williamson, *Markets and Hierarchies* (Free Press, 1983).

Given all the criticism that has been directed at the traditional hierarchical organization in the last fifteen to twenty years, it is easy to forget that it has served a purpose. For a large portion of the twentieth century, it has provided an effective solution to the informational constraints that technology—or the limits of technology—imposed on large enterprises.

The Japanese Corporation— Greater Richness, Less Reach

Today, Japanese management has lost some of its luster in the wake of the economic troubles plaguing that country, but Japanese corporations have often been praised by many observers as the major alternative to the traditional Western hierarchy.[1] They are still hierarchical: they have to be, because they work within the same informational constraints. But they make *significantly different trade-offs between richness and reach*.

The classic Japanese organization focuses more intently than does its Western counterpart on enhancing the richness of information flows. It achieves this higher level of richness through greater investment in those flows, and in some regards by sacrificing reach. In part these are organizational choices. In part they are reflections of the larger culture within which the Japanese corporation is embedded.[2] As a result, it represents a significant alternative to the Western corporation, based not on any superior use of information technology but on its different positioning along the richness/reach trade-off curve—a position that emphasizes richness more and reach less.

The most visible difference to the casual observer is the frequency and intimacy of physical *colocation*. In most Japanese companies, more managers are *colocated* in one building or complex of buildings and therefore are physically working together. White-collar companies, such as banks, have proven reluctant to move even part of their headquarters staff out of cramped and overpriced office space in the Otemachi and Marunouchi districts in central Tokyo, chiefly because of their concern to keep their staff together.[3] Within those buildings, walled-in offices are rare, even for quite senior executives: most white-collar workers sit at their desks in large, open rooms. Privacy is almost nonexistent.

A corollary of the culture of colocation is difficulty in dealing with geographic separation. Foreign postings are viewed by rising Japanese executives as mixed blessings because of the risk of separation from the "grapevine" back home. Japanese companies generally have greater discomfort than do their Western competitors in delegating decisions to their overseas operating subsidiaries. Non-Japanese executives fit awkwardly within the Japanese multinational hierarchy.

Within its bounded physical context, the Japanese corporation invests intensely in communication. Crisp, unilateral, high-level decision making is quite rare. Instead, decisions get made through a process of consensus building called *nemawashi*, which involves a wider range of individuals, and extends deeper down the hierarchy, than would be the case in Western companies. Plans are developed by teams that spend long periods of time working together, and participants are drawn from more areas, and more layers, of the organization. The origins of a proposal tend to become obscure; everyone becomes an "owner" by merit of having participated in the exhaustive discussion process. Near unanimity is a condition of action, and the final proposal is circulated for rubber-stamp approval only after exhaustive consultations, a process known as *ringi-seido*. Pressures on individuals or groups to go with the emerging consensus become intense.

Within the classic Japanese corporation, high performers rotate through a wide range of assignments. Senior managers thus acquire a broad exposure to their company, offset, perhaps, by less developed specialist skills. Rotation weakens sectional loyalties and intensifies loyalties to the corporation as a whole. This greater "reach" in career planning *within* the corporation is offset by lesser reach *across* corporations. The "classic" Japanese corporation offers, and expects, lifetime employment, at least from its male workers.[4] Lateral hiring has been very unusual. Dismissal or resignation is (or was until recently) a rare and shameful event.

High career fluidity laterally within the corporation and little fluidity across the corporate boundary together massively shape behavior. Corporate loyalty is very strong: employees know that they must work together for the duration of their professional lives. Individuals incur a high level of "reputation risk": any maneuver for short-term political advantage will be long remembered and eventually penalized. This transparency of employee actions limits opportunistic behavior and enhances trust. Trust then substitutes for the control that is emphasized in the Western hierarchy.

Investor relationships have many of the same characteristics as employee relationships: high richness and low reach. The major shareholders and creditors of the traditional

Japanese corporation are banks. Their investments tend to be large, and therefore illiquid, but Japanese banks have intimate involvement in corporate policy making and are represented on the board. These institutional investors lack the reach, in the form of liquidity, available to investors in Western organizations, but they enjoy a higher level of rich involvement in managerial information flows and decision making. Senior management responds to subtle signals from its large investors (and to administrative guidance from the powerful Finance Ministry and the Ministry of International Trade and Industry (MITI)), but investors outside this "club" are largely disenfranchised.

Mechanisms like these allow the Japanese corporation to achieve an intensely rich level of communication. But there is a price—the loss of reach, and the slowness and high cost of making decisions. Physical colocation, transparency of decision making, consensus, reputation risk, lifetime employment, and deep investor relationships all support rich flows of information, but can also produce parochialism, sluggishness, and incrementalism. Similarly, employees and investors enjoy security and have every motive to make the collective corporate enterprise work, but that motivation is predicated on the absence of real alternatives. Richness is bought at the expense of reach.

When compared to the traditional hierarchical model in the West, the Japanese model does derive significant advantages from its greater richness of communication. It is better at identifying opportunities for incremental improvements. It is better at combining the talents of many people, each of whom has a small contribution to make. It is better at mobilizing human resources around a single goal. It is better at reviewing its own learning processes and then improving them.

In some respects, however, the Japanese corporation is at a disadvantage. Processes that require extensive involvement by a wide range of people limit the ability of the organization to make crisp changes in strategic direction. The lack of individual reward may discourage innovation. Pressure to conform to the prevailing consensus may discourage creative thinking.

As the ambiguous history of the past two decades illustrates, it is not obvious that either system is superior to the other (or that either could be comprehensively transplanted from one society to the other). They just make different trade-offs between richness and reach in the key information flows. Power relations, trust, mobility, equity, incentive, and adaptability are all reconfigured in consequence.

But the traditional Western corporation and the traditional Japanese corporation really resemble each other far more than they differ. They are positioned on the same, technologically determined, richness/reach trade-off curve (though at different points). They are both hierarchical and hard-wired, permanent, and largely impermeable. Both are therefore potential targets for deconstruction.

Deconstructing Ownership, Risk Bearing, and Control

The deconstruction of corporate ownership occurred over time, and its story is largely familiar. Capital markets connected investors with enterprises, and financial instruments served as the standards defining investment contracts. This pushed out the trade-off between richness and reach for investors: they can enjoy a rich understanding of risks and potential returns without having to restrict their investments

to a small number of proprietorships. Recent advances in connectivity and standards continue to push out the richness/
reach trade-off of corporate ownership.

Initially, the enterprise was owned by an individual or
perhaps a family—capital, risk, power, and control all were
vested in the same hands. With the explosion of industrial
scale, ownership grew into partnerships, and then into joint-
stock companies, allowing multiple people to have a stake in
the company without actually controlling it; and those stakes
could be bought and sold on stock markets. This was the first
deconstruction of the ownership relationship. It made corporate ownership liquid and allowed for many financing possibilities. And it separated ownership from control, allowing
the development of the managerial class.

The corporation, and the legal system within which it
flourished, developed a set of mechanisms to provide its
numerous and distant owners with the information they
needed to make investment decisions. Outside directors. The
annual report. Accounting standards. The independent audit.
In a looser sense, financial journalism, stock analysts, and
professional money managers evolved as "navigators"
through the thicket of qualitative factors that influence
investment decisions. Corporate debt evolved in similar
ways. Loans, and later bonds, deconstructed the risk-bearing
function of capital markets into the structured risk of the
lender or bondholder and the residual risk borne by the
shareholder, thus allowing different investors to bear different kinds of risk. Standards, in the form of covenants, bank-
ruptcy obligations, and bond ratings, combined with the
connectivity provided by capital markets to allow corporate
debt ownership to deconstruct.

The securitization and fragmentation of ownership
appeared for a long time to be taking control of the corporation away from owners and placing it in the hands of a man-

agerial hierarchy answerable to no one.[5] However, the hostile takeover has deconstructed the fixed relation between the corporate assets and the managerial team. There is now a robust "market for corporate control," and any management that fails to extract from a corporation its maximum value is vulnerable to summary displacement. So not only is ownership fragmented and risk disaggregated, but even the entrepreneurial function itself is contingent on the ability of management to justify its performance.

Today, deconstruction continues to extend into ownership, risk bearing, and control. Factoring, leasing, and the sale of receivables allow companies to move whole classes of assets and risks off their balance sheets and onto those of institutions better able to carry them. Securitization of financial assets such as mortgages and automotive and credit card receivables has allowed financial institutions to concentrate on originating, processing, or holding the loan: a "deconstruction" of the integrated lending business of thirty years ago. This deconstruction is facilitated by the liquidity of the markets (reach) and standards that define risk and return for the various pools of loans (richness).

Deconstruction is also materializing in the deliberate breakup of integrated ownership. The recognition of a "conglomerate discount" led many companies to spin off unrelated businesses so that investors could own deconstructed "pure plays" (for example, GM selling Hughes Electronics). Companies believing that certain assets were undervalued because they were buried within a larger corporation have performed partial spin-offs, sufficient to establish an independent stock price for those assets without losing control. Thermo-Electron has made itself famous by defining spin-off as a reward for success: operating managers are "incented" with shadow equity in their division, which turns into real equity if the operation is successful enough to be sold.[6]

In the world of startups, the venture capitalist's portfolio is a deconstructed alternative to the corporate structure. Venture capitalists specialize in evaluating plans and people. They broker technologies, make introductions, and help recruit the managerial team. They provide capital but shift a lot of risk bearing (and therefore incentive) back onto the shoulders of management. They clean up the mess if businesses fail. Above all, and in contrast to corporations, they see ownership as *transient* and in no sense the essence of their business: a successful investment is liquidated as soon as it becomes more attractive to a corporate buyer or to the capital markets.

These trends will continue. Capital provision, risk bearing, and control are logically separable functions. Within each function, we can distinguish different kinds of investment, different pools of risk, and multiple facets of power. The world becomes more efficient as different players focus on different functions, in accordance with their competitive advantage. But deconstructing these functions requires *standards*: for information exchange, for contracts, and for the measurement of risk and return. And these standards, like all other standards, need critical mass—what in the financial world is called "liquidity."

Connectivity is one requirement for liquidity, and this connectivity already exists: participants in capital markets are connected by modern technology. But liquidity is really driven by the number of players *evaluating* a transaction, rather than the number actually transacting. Advances in technology allow investors to analyze and make decisions on *orders-of-magnitude* more potential transactions today than was possible just ten years ago. The liquidity of capital markets, when measured by players evaluating transactions, is growing at a rate proportional to Moore's Law. Although this does not guarantee the evolution of standards or further deconstruction of ownership and risk bearing, it makes them much more likely.

Deconstructing Employment

The depth and sophistication of modern capital markets explains why the deconstruction of ownership and risk bearing has already progressed. Labor markets are much less sophisticated, but the same thing is occurring: an enormous explosion in richness and reach.

Most obviously, the spread of Internet connectivity and the proliferation of electronic marketplaces for jobs are beginning to impact the broader labor market, particularly for managerial and professional jobs. Most newspaper Help Wanted sections are posted in parallel on the paper's Web site. Internet-only job marketplaces, such as Careers.com, are growing faster than any other category of classified electronic advertising. The majority of large corporations use their Web sites as a gateway for job seekers, and for many professional firms, the primary purpose of their Web presence is actually recruiting. Among college seniors, evaluating potential employers by digging around on the Net has become standard practice. A 1997 survey by the American Management Association found that 53 percent of major companies were filling job openings via the Internet, and the director of the Career Center at Stanford University predicts that within five years 95 percent of all jobs will be posted on the Net.[7] Moreover, the usual advantages of hyperlinks and electronic customization enable on-line listing services to include the rich information that potential applicants would require when considering job options, such as compensation, cost of living, schools, and housing. Easy access enables employed people to keep their toes in the labor market; people are becoming much more informed about their external employability, prevailing pay rates, and the specific alternatives to their current job. Employees now easily and anonymously can track information that previously was accessible only through a dedicated search. The information asymmetry goes away.

But deconstruction of labor markets extends far beyond merely lubricating the job search. In some labor markets we are witnessing a shift to more *continuously market-based relationships* between employer and employee. The cost of *switching* jobs is dropping as information asymmetries and the cost of searching drop. As with capital markets, this increasing "liquidity" in the job market allows individuals to bear risk: if one job doesn't work out, try another. The explosion of freelancing, aided often by telecommuting, is a direct consequence.[8]

This extreme pattern can most clearly be seen in geographically concentrated, talent-based industries—industries in which labor rather than capital creates value, skill levels are high but not specific to a given employer, and geographic concentration allows for high mobility. In these industries, we find all the characteristics of deconstruction: an explosion of reach through connectivity and standards, a melting of the glue bonding employee to employer, the substitution of fluid, collaborative networks for static hierarchy, and a "de-averaging" of the patterns of reward.

On Wall Street, for example, traders create substantial value. They do basically the same job in one firm as they do in another, and they can move from one employer to another with ease because so many of the firms are in such close proximity. Individual performance is easy to measure in terms of trading profits: the reputation of "stars" spreads quickly. Stars are impossible to replicate. Ease of exit (reach) and the existence of common performance standards force an otherwise hierarchical relation to operate on an arms-length market basis. The top performers must be paid their economic value; otherwise they will quit. There is little leeway to pay traders based on seniority, "fairness," or other criteria valued by hierarchical organizations. Traders' loyalty lies with their profession (or with themselves), but not really with their employer. "Promotion" is not much of an incentive for conformity. The value of skills, whether innate or acquired on the job, accrues to the individual. The business may require lots of capital, but capital is less scarce than skill. It is therefore quite difficult for the investor to extract much return from owning part of a successful trading operation: too much of the value is extracted by those who create it.

Hollywood has evolved similarly. At the height of the studio system in the 1940s, stars were created by the promotional efforts of the studios, who held them under exclusive contract and were able to extract the bulk of the value of the "brands" they had thereby created. However, through the fifties and sixties this structure broke down, as the absolute value of "talent," enormous disparities in that value, and the *visibility* of those disparities to all the participants became progressively more apparent. Agents and lawyers began negotiating shorter and nonexclusive contracts for their clients. As the liquidity of the talent market rose, stars were able to extract more and more of the value they created. Today most of the value from a film accrues to the "talent," be it producer, director, or actor. Stars are becoming more like entrepreneurs: they receive a percentage of the gross, or participate in ad hoc partnerships, which bear much of the risk. The studios, like trading houses, serve as utilities.

The professional sports industry has passed through the same evolution for much the same reasons. There was a time when major sports events were the biggest sources of profitability to the television networks. Through aggressive contract negotiations (aided by the proliferation of competing networks), that value was extracted by the sports leagues. But with the advent of free agency, the clubs in turn were held hostage by their star players, to whom the real value has ultimately accrued. Star value extends beyond the playing field, and so does the deconstructive logic. Michael Jordan's name was used brilliantly by Nike to market the Air Jordan line of athletic shoes. But Nike was caught off guard when Jordan announced his first retirement. The firm realized how important he was to the Nike business, and it allowed Jordan to have his own shoe brand. Nike was forced to accept Jordan's terms, including the exclusion of the word Nike from what is now the Jordan brand.[9] Whatever the relative contributions historically, Jordan was now able to extract his exit value from the business by merit of the visibility and portability of his contribution.

In all of these industries, the key unit of value creation is the *individual*, and that value is largely independent of the team within which that individual works.[10] The value created can be known to potential as well as current employers, the individual can create as much value in one employment context as another, and costs of switching are low relative to the rewards that can thereby be gained. The tightness of the industry—navigated by headhunters, talent scouts, agents, lawyers, and intense personal networking—facilitates connectivity. Standards for measuring performance and defining the terms and duration of contracts facilitate comparability and job switching.

When the employment contract deconstructs, issues of parity and of moving in lockstep with one's colleagues—so important in the hierarchical organization and still more so in the Japanese organization—are cast aside. Loyalty tends to be defined in terms of the professional cadre to which one belongs rather than to the particular employer for whom one is currently working. And the logic of deconstructing value chains is carried to its limit: individual employees (the smallest possible sliver of the business) extract the value that they uniquely create.

Comprehensive Deconstruction: Silicon Valley

The clearest example of simultaneously deconstructing labor and capital markets is Silicon Valley. Initially, policy makers worried that the fragmented structure of the Californian electronics industry would handicap it against the greater scale and capacity for strategic resource allocation of large competitors on the East Coast and in Asia. Now it is celebrated as a new model of industrial organization (see Figure 10-1).

Workers in the Valley are extraordinarily mobile: studies have found turnover rates of over 35 percent in local electronics firms and as high as 59 percent in the smallest firms. Average job tenure is about two years.[11] This is possible because skills at all levels tend to be specific to the region but not to any one company within it. People also share a common background: most are electrical engineers, many are graduates of the engineering schools at Stanford and Berkeley, and in the early days, many were alumni of one firm: Fairchild Semiconductor. Loyalties reflect this. As one executive remarked: "Here in Silicon Valley there's far greater loyalty to one's craft than to one's company. A company is just a vehicle which allows you to work."[12] Homogeneity and colocation facilitate labor force fluidity.

Homogeneity and colocation also support community. Professional and alumni organizations, after-hours socializing at favorite watering holes, and the friendships built as careers cross and recross all support a pattern of dense local

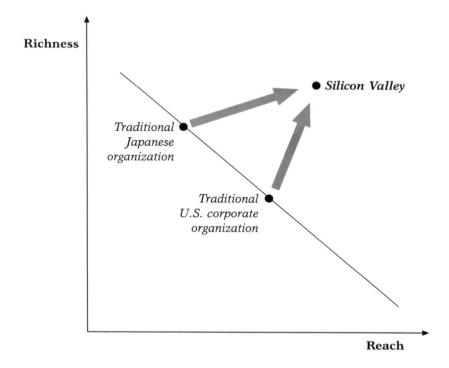

Figure 10-1: Organization: Blowing Up the Richness/Reach Trade-off

networking. This creates a high measure of *transparency:* reputations are built across the entire community and reputation risk, much as within the Japanese corporation, shapes behavior. The fact that a competitor one day may be a colleague the next, that the role of boss and the role of subordinate are interchangeable, sustains a regional culture that balances competitive and collaborative values.

Venture capitalists play a parallel role in allocating and reallocating labor, capital, and technology. Their expertise tends to be more technical than financial. Since multiple investors are typically involved in each firm, they, too, compete and collaborate simultaneously.

The result is a business environment characterized by porous company boundaries. Firms cannot lock in their investors or their employees; they have the greatest difficulty in locking in technologies and know-how. But while every firm individually may see these as problems, in the aggregate they gain as much from the people, funds, or knowledge they absorb as they lose from any leakage. Porosity stimulates the capacity for innovation more than it dissipates the motivation.

Individual firms come and go—temporary alliances of people pursuing specific, narrowly defined projects. The more permanent reality is the fluid business "ecosystem" within which those firms compete. In some ways, Silicon Valley performs as a large, decentralized corporation. The Valley, not its constituent firms, owns the labor pool. The Valley, through its venture capital community, starts projects, terminates them, and allocates capital among them. The Valley, not its constituent firms, is the real locus of core competencies. Because of the ease of diversification it affords to investors and employees, it is the Valley collectively that absorbs much of the burden of risk.[13]

As a "corporation," Silicon Valley has eclipsed the traditional hierarchical corporations of Route 128 in Boston. It has also outperformed the immensely aggressive and competent corporations of Japan. It has done so without a finance department or a human resources department. It has done so without a corporate strategy. And without a CEO.

Silicon Valley has the internal mobility and rich transparency of a Japanese corporation, allowing it to achieve high levels of trust and collaboration. But it also has the accountability of the traditional Western hierarchical organization. And it offers the direct relationship between initiative, innovation, and reward that is found in open markets. The blowup of the traditional trade-offs between richness and reach, for employees and for investors simultaneously, enables modes of collaboration and initiative that capture some of the best features of all the traditional organizational models.

Wider Implications

Is this just a special case? Silicon Valley works because of geographic concentration, skill intensity, homogeneity, and the sophistication of its workers and investors. It also works because of *success*: growth and the possibility of huge capital gains lubricate and energize the entire system. Most businesses are very different.

But, as we have repeatedly argued, it doesn't matter what "most" businesses are like: if *slivers* of the business would compete more effectively under a Silicon Valley structure, then they in isolation will become objects for deconstruction. (Those slivers are quite likely, of course, to account for most of the value of the business.) Drug companies may be huge brand- and distribution-driven companies, but *if* the research function could operate better under a different model, the fact that manufacturing and sales force management require hierarchy and control is quite irrelevant. It simply makes the case for managing the two parts of the business differently, and possibly independently. Indeed, the increasing role of independent pharmaceutical and biotech research companies suggests that this is precisely what is beginning to happen.

The limitation of geographic proximity is very real today. However, extranets like ANX are moving quite rapidly in the direction of displacing the trade-off between richness and physical reach. Broadband communication will enhance the richness of distant collaboration.[14] Many executives and commentators are already speculating about the possibilities

Frequently Asked Questions

1. **Which parts of my organization are most suscepti-
   ble to deconstruction?**

   The high-skill, knowledge-intensive pieces. The pieces
   where individual skills matter most. The pieces where
   collective skills benefit most from exposure to the widest
   possible universe of practitioners. The pieces that make
   a disproportionate contribution to the value of the
   business.

2. **Doesn't porosity of boundaries mean that the corporation never gets a return on its investment? If so,
   why bother to invest?**

   This is a real dilemma. If companies were perfectly
   "leaky" in ideas or skills, that would destroy their motive
   to invest; if they were perfectly "watertight" there would
   be none of the benefits of participating in a business "ecosystem." In fact they are *somewhat* leaky, and the balance
   seems to work. Knight Ridder, faced with the digitization
   of the information business, has chosen to move its headquarters from Miami to San Jose, seeking the benefits of
   participation in Silicon Valley, but incurring a real risk
   that its best ideas, people, and skills will leak to startup
   competitors. Kodak, faced with the digitization of photog-
   raphy, has rejected that option and chosen to stay in
   Rochester, New York. Knight Ridder probably got it right.

of virtual teaming.[15] Nobody knows how far this can go,
how far friendship, trust, moral obligation, and the rich
human connection of professional relationships can evolve
remotely. But we should not exclude it, especially if the
reward is Silicon Valley levels of performance.

Deconstructed capital markets, deconstructed labor mar-kets, and the multiplicative consequences of deconstructing both simultaneously pose fundamental challenges to the tra-ditional organizational models of West and East. They open up an organizational alternative somewhere between mar-kets and hierarchies, an alternative that may achieve much of the richness of the former together with the reach of the latter. How far, how soon, how comprehensively this new model will penetrate into the realities of practical manage-ment are genuine uncertainties. But it is hard to deny that these questions are now on the table.

The Organizational Response

Deconstructed capital markets and deconstructed labor mar-kets together challenge the idea that the corporation really owns its competitive advantages. They suggest a view of the firm as a *manifestation* of competencies and competitive advantages whose true source is individuals or the "ecosys-tem" within which the firm is embedded. They further sug-gest that fluid, self-organizing collaboration can succeed without the traditional infrastructure of hierarchy, control, and leadership. The Silicon Valley model emerges, offering reach beyond that of the conventional organization and rich-ness beyond that of the conventional market. Not a model for all business, quite obviously, but a model for the skill- and knowledge-intensive parts where profits are made.

Microsoft, by far the most successful corporation of the past twenty years, has defeated one conventional competi-tive threat after another. But its greatest long-term vulnera-bility, in the opinion of some commentators, is to a loose federation of software designers called the Open Software Alliance. Collaborating worldwide on the basis of an agreed

The Object-Oriented Organization

Modern software is built from "objects": complex pieces of self-contained code, composed of both instructions and data. Each object has a specific task and calls up other objects for help as needed. Any object, in principle, can invoke any other: objects can be organized and reorganized in whatever way makes sense for the task at hand. The art of object definition is the art of capturing knotty complexities that require complex logic internally but simple connections with the rest of the computational universe. Objects are modular: each can be removed and replaced without affecting any others. Object-oriented programming is massively inefficient in terms of traditional metrics such as computation cycles and lines of code. But the ease of updating the pieces, and of recombining the pieces for new purposes, outweighs considerations of static efficiency. Object-oriented programming is an architecture that maximizes *adaptability*.

Teams are the "objects" of the new organization. They too are recombinant and modular. To perform any fixed task, they are invariably less efficient than the hard-wired division of labor of the traditional hierarchy. But as the richness/reach trade-off shifts, that static inefficiency costs less, and as the pace of competition accelerates, their superior *adaptability* counts for more.

By becoming "object-oriented" the organization is able to operate at higher levels of complexity, preserve a culture of collaboration, and achieve degrees of adaptability heretofore available only to markets.

on and evolving set of standards, members of the alliance have produced an operating system called LINUX that many regard as the best available. It's already used on seven million desktops worldwide. And it is free. But if something as amorphous as the Open Software Alliance really is the most serious threat to a company as strong as Microsoft, what does that imply for everybody else?

Part of the answer is that organizations can and must compete by acting like the deconstructed models that challenge them. Part lies in the fact that there are *still* important things that individual organizations can do better than amorphous environments such as Silicon Valley, and that organizations must focus their scope and competitive advantage on precisely those types of activity.

Acting "Deconstructed"

Organizations are responding to new competitive challenges by mimicking many of the characteristics of deconstructed organizational environments. *Internally* they are exploiting connectivity and standards to support the fluid, self-organizing flows of talent, technology, and capital that we traditionally associate with markets. *Externally* they are exploiting rich connectivity to support the deep collaboration, shared competencies, and common strategies that we traditionally associate with organizations. The traditional distinction between internal hierarchy and external markets becomes blurred.[16]

Within the organization, for example, many corporations are installing companywide standards to measure performance and allocate capital in ways that closely approximate those of capital markets. They are adopting shareholder valuation methods that allow measurement of each business unit's notional contribution to the corporation's stock price. These methods, in turn, make it possible to reward divisional managers as owners of the "company" that they control.[17]

Risk is shifted onto their shoulders, together with new possibilities for the creation of personal wealth.

Conversely, *among* corporations, alliances are proliferating. Corporations have found ways to engage in open-ended collaboration in research, design, and logistics. Companies ally to pool complementary competencies. They collaborate to define industrywide standards for products or technologies, especially in areas where innovations will succeed only if a critical mass of users adopts them. They compete and collaborate with each other at the same time.

At a deeper level, the response to deconstruction lies less in performance standards and alliances, and more in emerging cultural and managerial norms of the organization. These will be dominated by three characteristics: *fluidity, flatness,* and *trust.*

Fluidity

The "hard-wired" structure of the conventional corporate organization reflects the high cost of establishing information channels. But as these costs fall, the organization can become "soft-wired." People can group and regroup into teams. Individuals can participate in multiple projects simultaneously. People within a team can work out roles and responsibilities without much managerial direction. Teams in turn can team. They can merge for some common purpose and then segregate. Just as roles substitute for fixed job descriptions, so teams substitute for fixed departments. Neither roles nor teams have any permanence. Organization becomes continuously self-organizing and adapting. The organization builds competitive advantage not from what it is or does, but from how it reviews, learns from, and then amends its own procedures and structure.[18]

Flatness

Spans of control are proportional to reach. Double the span of control, all else being equal, and you halve the management layers needed in an organization. Authority is never eliminated, since strategy is still required, but the number of tiers in the hierarchy can be radically reduced. More important than a flattening of the formal organizational structure is the flattening of the informal channels for sharing, reassuring, lobbying, and coaching, which is where senior managers often have their greatest impact. The art of steering an organization by means of multiple informal interventions, rather than formal plans and reviews, becomes a hallmark of new organizational leadership. Managing by e-mail rather than managing by meetings.

Trust

Greater richness and reach imply greater symmetry of information. When information is richer and can flow freely across an organization, everyone's actions become more transparent. As with the Japanese corporation, the importance of *reputation risk* increases. Disgruntled subordinates and poor performance are harder to hide. Managerial successes become known without having to be trumpeted. As information symmetry and reputation risk increase, employees are more strongly motivated to be good corporate citizens, placing (and being *seen* to place) the collective interest above their parochial concerns. As is true of social communities, transparency puts the corporation in a position to expect and obtain a higher level of collaboration among its members.[19] Reputation substitutes for formal mechanisms of review and control.

These three implications—fluidity, flatness, and trust—are fundamental ingredients of a new organizational model. But they are shifts in degree, not kind. Elements of structure, hierarchy, and information asymmetry always remain.

As organizations adopt these practices internally, a certain "fractal" pattern emerges. People collaborate fluidly within teams. Teams collaborate fluidly within corporations. Corporations collaborate fluidly within the business "ecosystem." At all levels, the smaller unit sustains greater richness internally, but achieves reach through the context provided by the larger unit. At all levels, organization and information channels are recombinant and soft-wired. At all levels, transparency sustains trust. At all levels, richness sustains collaboration, and reach enables competition.

SOUND BITS

- There have been two organizational debates: markets versus hierarchies; and within hierarchies, the Western model versus the Japanese. New combinations of richness and reach are allowing new organizational forms that combine the best of all structures.

- Business "ecosystems" are limited by the fact that distance constrains richness, but *only* by that fact. That constraint will go away. The question is not whether, the question is *when*.

- If information is symmetric, trust substitutes for control.

- Organization within the firm and organization across firms are increasingly becoming variants on exactly the same thing. This makes the boundaries of the corporation fuzzy and indeterminate.

- Organization at large scale and organization at small scale are increasingly becoming variants on exactly the same thing. Individuals, teams, businesses, and corporations all interact on the basis of flatness, fluidity, and trust.

- Cooperation and competition, collaboration and initiative, richness and reach can all coexist, everywhere.

11

mONDay mORNINg

$\mathbf{m}$UCH OF MANAGEMENT is about concreteness and tactics—stepwise solutions to prioritized, practical problems. Deconstruction, in contrast, presents a dizzying degree of fluidity, indeterminacy, and instability. It is the opposite of what most managers are trained to deal with. That makes it discomforting. It is mentally exhausting. One craves a simple forecast, straightforward prescriptions, a specific set of "to do's" for Monday morning.

That is really difficult. Deconstruction is not a new set of rules about strategy; it is an argument that all the old rules of strategy apply, but at a much finer level of granularity. With the partial exception of pure information businesses, the strategies themselves are essentially the same: scale, market share, cost, innovation, capabilities, competencies, and the rest. But the *objects* of those strategies are different. And the task is therefore one of identifying these new objects and then rethinking and reapplying the same old principles of competitive advantage.

There are no shortcuts to doing this, no simple, across-the-board substitutes for hard thinking about business specifics. However, we would like to suggest a dozen *guiding principles* that may help with the task of rethinking strategy in an era of deconstruction.

Some Guiding Principles

1. *No business leader today can presume that the business definitions in his or her business will still be valid a few years from now.*

   Deconstruction means that traditional business definitions can no longer be taken for granted. Suppliers, customers, competitors, industry, value chain, supply chain, consumer franchise, and relations with employees and owners all become *variables*; they are reshaped by the shifting economics of information and by the strategies pursued by players who exploit those economics. Moreover, the process of deconstruction is continual. Driven by connectivity and standards, progressive advances in richness and reach will challenge successive business definitions with the possibilities of further deconstruction. There is no endgame.

2. *Deconstruction is most likely to strike in precisely those parts of the business where incumbents have most to lose and are least willing to recognize it.*

   It is easy to deny the importance of deconstruction by pointing out some central and possibly large part of the business that will *not* be deconstructed: the patient-physician relationship, the investor's need for human reassurance, brand loyalty, the requirement in the factory for hierarchical control. But management is not about being a custodian of assets, it is about *creating value.*

The new opportunities for value creation lie where the underlying economics are shifting; managers need to focus on these opportunities. And the products, segments, or functions where the economics are shifting are likely to be precisely the areas where disproportionate value is created. So concentrate on playing the deconstruction game to create *new* value.

3. *Waiting for someone else to demonstrate the feasibility of deconstruction hands over the biggest advantage a competitor could possibly wish for: time.*

In Internet time, everything is a sprint. It is easy to deny deconstruction by pointing to a history of failures by those who have tried. This is really dangerous. When preemption matters and new businesses evolve at breakneck speed, then the first competitor to get it right will have an enormous advantage. *By definition*, that first competitor ignored the evidence of a prior, unbroken series of failures.

"Fast follower" strategies may work in marathons, but not in sprints.

4. *Leaders need to wrestle with the full range of possible patterns of deconstruction.*

Businesses can be deconstructed in four possible ways. Some will break up into discrete components of their value chain, unlinked by the melting of the informational glue that bonded them together. Others will deconstruct along their vertical links with suppliers, customers, and consumers, when mutual relationships, stable franchises, and intermediary roles are undermined by reach. Others will see the segregation of information flows into businesses in their own right. Still others will deconstruct in their organizational relations, as employees, investors, and entrepreneurs renegotiate roles, risks, and rewards.

These deconstructions may be partial or they may be comprehensive. They are not mutually exclusive. They are often mutually interdependent. No successful strategy in the face of deconstruction can ignore any of these patterns.

5. *Strategy really matters.*

    In a world of stability, strategy is applied economics: refining segmentation, disaggregating costs, optimizing features, and the like. It is a *response* to supply- and demand-side realities that exist quite independently of the ability of the business leader to figure them out. But in a deconstructing world, strategy creates economic realities. Whether a standard does or does not reach critical mass, who preempts whom, and who allies with whom, determine not just the path of competitive jockeying, but the end result itself. The interplay of strategies among competitors has an autonomous impact in shaping the outcome.

6. *The value of winning will escalate, as will the cost of losing.*

    As a result of unbundling, the economics of businesses after deconstruction will often be simpler and therefore more powerful: competitive advantage and the distribution of rewards will become much more skewed. Information flows, in particular, will tend to become either valueless or monopolies, and it *really matters* to understand which. If, within a given business, there is room for only one winner, getting strategy *right* becomes really important: *getting it right becomes more important than not getting it wrong.* Therefore, do some very "uncorporate" things: experiment, preempt, pursue contrary strategies simultaneously.

7. *The reconstructed business definitions will rarely correspond to the old.*

New businesses will emerge and agglomerate in accordance with their own competitive logic. Emerging information businesses will spill across the boundaries of the physical businesses from which they originate. Successful competitors will therefore have to build or acquire fundamentally new capabilities, make alliances with companies in previously unrelated businesses, and merge aggressively for preemptive scale and scope. Underestimating the requirement for acquiring new capabilities and overestimating the value of existing capabilities is a common trap.

8. *The hardest step for an incumbent organization is the mental one of seeing the business through a different, deconstructed lens and then acting on this insight.*

Mentally deconstructing the business sounds easy in theory, but as soon as the practical implications become clear, the reaction of every organization is resistance. A "navigator" strategy sounds terrific, up to the point where being the best navigator requires navigating to competitors' products. A "preemptive" strategy sounds heroic, until a succession of premature failures and the dilution of corporate earnings hit the income statement. A "disintermediating" strategy sounds great, until the dealers revolt. *That* is when the incumbent blinks and the insurgent steals an unmerited but devastating advantage.

9. *The subtler pitfall is co-option and passive resistance by a skeptical and self-preserving organization.*

Organizations have an uncanny ability to subvert whatever undermines their historical structures of power and reward, even when the new direction is the official strategy. The IT Department takes years to build an "industrial strength" Web interface; the sales force takes charge of the "smooth transition" to the new distribution channel; the rewards for entrepreneurship are set in accordance with established corporate HR policies. All mistakes.

Intending, doubtless, to leverage its core competencies, Westinghouse assigned the new "transistor" business to its Vacuum Tube Division. In consequence it killed in one stroke its best hope for the future of the company.

10. *Strategy in a deconstructing world has to be generally right, but need not be specifically right, as long as the organization maintains a capacity to learn from its mistakes.*

Strategy in a deconstructing world cannot be planned in the same ways as in the past. Planning presumes certainty, or at least bounded uncertainty. It presumes that the numbers can be analyzed, the payoffs identified. It posits milestones, budgets, cash flows, accountabilities. The entire system of corporate planning is designed to avoid error. But in conditions of high uncertainty, error is inevitable and people unwilling to make mistakes will get it right *too late* to claim any reward for their meticulousness. Strategizing has to be *continuous;* it has to be partially *improvisational;* it has to be flexible enough to recognize errors when they have occurred, correct them, and *move on.*

11. *The value of incumbents' best assets is all too often destroyed by the organizational, behavioral, and personal baggage that they insist on bringing to the new venture.*

IT people struggle with a terrible headache called "legacy systems": enormous information architectures, with layer upon layer of improvements, extensions, and investments, that turn out to be massively inferior to a simple, clean, new box. Beyond a certain point, the problems of updating and maintaining compatibility become so severe that it makes sense to junk the entire system and start from scratch. Business systems are *human* software: they follow exactly the same logic. There are legacy organizations, legacy mindsets, legacy competencies. And beyond a certain point it is necessary to junk *them* and start again.

Current corporate planning procedures are likely to *subtract* value in the way they deal with deconstruction. Traditional expertise on marketing or product development may be not only irrelevant, but dangerously misleading. Homegrown career executives may have exactly the wrong skills and attitudes. Undiluted corporate ownership may prove an untenable way to distribute responsibility and rewards.

So the imperative of new strategies implies the imperative of new processes.

12. *Incumbents can be the insurgents, if they choose.*

Incumbents do not have to think of themselves as incumbents: that is to presume precisely the static business and industry definitions that deconstruction denies. They can take some capability of theirs right into the heart of somebody else's business and *blow it up.* It takes clarity of vision and consistency of purpose. It requires organizing and rewarding differently, perhaps even owning differently.

The devastating truth is that for the vast majority of deconstruction opportunities that have emerged to date, *some large corporation was actually the best positioned to exploit it.* Almost invariably it failed to do so, and a few young entrepreneurs became billionaires in consequence. It failed to do so because it failed to think like insurgents: it was not aggressive enough; it was not *greedy* enough. It was still studying the situation.

Leadership

In a deconstructing world, the traditional, hierarchically defined roles of leadership become obsolete. But there remain two things that leaders, and only leaders, can do.

The first is creating a *culture.* Common cultures obviously emerge from the environments from which the corporation is drawn: national, regional, and professional. But the unique cultural values that a corporation builds on top of that are conscious and deliberate *creations.* They reflect the vision of a leader. They are established through incentives, through the selection of other leaders, and above all *by example.*

Defining culture and prescribing how to build it are beyond the scope of this book. But whatever the richness embedded in this vague but crucial word, it applies uniquely and specifically within the bounds of the corporation. It thus embeds a richness/reach trade-off, one that cannot be displaced by technology, and that survives, indeed thrives, on the shift from hierarchy to fluidity, flatness, and trust. As other sources of structure and apparent stability prove ephemeral, as business boundaries and organizational structures melt into transience, the rich culture of the organization—if it has one—becomes a precious asset. *The* precious asset. Culture, not factories, brands, business definitions, or patterns of ownership, defines the corporation. And that is uniquely the creation of leadership.

The second task of leadership is *strategy*. There are always small moves, experiments, improvements: things that an organization with the right capabilities and motivation will do for itself. But there are also *big moves*. Deconstruction screams out for big moves, just as it frees the strategist from the traditional limitations of business definition and ownership structure. In this environment, as in no other, the smart and the bold will outfox the slow and the cautious. It is the leader's skill in making those big moves, second only to her skill in building the right culture, that will make the difference between success and oblivion.

Theorists have variously seen the corporation as a set of physical assets, a set of property rights, or a body of core competencies. Those can all be deconstructed. What *resists* deconstruction is the idea of the corporation as defined by its culture and its strategy. The corporation as *purposeful community*. And if all else fades, perhaps purposeful community becomes the essence of identity, of management, of leadership. In a world of impersonal technical change, that is a refreshingly human thought.

endnotes

chapter one

1. Richard A. Melcher, "Dusting Off the Britannica," *BusinessWeek*, 20 October 1997, 143.

2. Ibid.

3. "Slow-to-Adapt Encyclopedia Britannica Is for Sale," *New York Times*, 16 May 1995, 1.

4. The GDP statistics analyzed by economists would capture neither the drop in price nor any quality changes in the shift from print to electronic encyclopedias over this period. This illustrates the irrelevance of much of the macroeconomic debates over the impact or non-impact of information technology on "productivity." It also illustrates the peculiar propensity of economists to interpret their inability to measure something as a statement about the world as opposed to a statement about economists (c.f. the "efficient markets hypothesis" in finance). For the purposes of the arguments of this book, however, it does not matter whether the substitution of CD-ROMs for multivolume printed products (or any other manifestation of the new economics of information) is deemed (or measured as) economic progress or not. The substitution has a tremendous effect on *competitive advantage*, and that, not GDP, is the focus of our argument.

chapter two

1. Boston Consulting Group, "Managing for a Wired Health Care Industry," *INVIVO*, July/August 1996.

2. An automotive executive estimated to one of the authors that in 1999 GM will ship more MIPS than IBM.

3. The classic study of the origins of large-scale organization is Alfred D. Chandler, Jr., *Strategy and Structure: Chapters in the History of the American Industrial Enterprise* (Cambridge: MIT Press, 1962).

4. There is more to organization than information channels: notably power and the bearing of risk. However, these in turn are grounded in informational logic. We return to this in chapter 10.

5. The fact that information channels are a glue linking value chains, supply chains, consumer franchises, and organizations together does not imply that they are the *only* glue. Physical colocation of supplier and customer, the physical compatibility of one product with another, and costs of physically switching from one product or service to another can also be glues that bond players together, and they are unrelated to information. However, with falling transportation costs, interchangeable parts, flexible production, and a host of other innovations, physical specificity is diminishing in importance. Moreover, such physical factors generally explain only "small-scale" vertical integration. The larger-scale links that we call value and supply chains are much more likely to be bonded by information. Physical specificity, in other words, may explain why a tool and a die are owned and operated together, but does not in general explain why a car assembler also owns component manufacturing capacity.

6. Since SABRE is now a separately quoted company, we can directly compare the values of the information and the physical businesses. At the time of writing, SABRE has a market value of $7.8 billion, and AMR (the parent of American Airlines) is valued at $11 billion. Since AMR owns 82% of SABRE, the implicit valuation of American Airlines (together with its commuter operation, American Eagle) is therefore $4.6 billion. SABRE, the information business, is thus worth nearly *double* the physical airline business it was originally created to support. In an even more extreme example, Priceline.com, an Internet marketplace for airline tickets whose losses are three times its revenues, was valued at $10 billion in its April 1999 public offering. Rightly or

wrongly, this is greater than the combined values of United, Northwest, and Continental airlines.

7. See George Stalk, Philip Evans, and Lawrence E. Shulman. "Competing on Capabilities: The New Rules of Corporate Strategy," *Harvard Business Review*, March–April 1992.

8. "A senior Coca-Cola executive is said to have declared that the company could survive the loss of all its plants, capital, staff, and access to raw materials, providing that it kept possession of the Coca-Cola logo. With that it would be possible to walk into a bank and receive sufficient credit to replace the entire global infrastructure." Patrick Parrinder, review of *The Cultural Life of Intellectual Properties,* by Rosemary J. Coombe, in *The Times Literary Supplement,* March 12, 1999, p. 11.

9. IDC/LINK 1998 U.S. Household survey, pp.1, 29.

10. Linda Himelstein, Heather Green, Richard Siklos, and Catherine Yang, "Yahoo! The Company, The Strategy, The Stock," *Business-Week,* 7 September 1998, p. 66. The television show in question was *ER.*

11. International Data Corporation Web site: < www.idc.com >.

12. Christopher Mines, "Broadband Hits Home," *Forrester Research* report, 2 August 1998.

13. International Data Corporation Web site: < www.idc.com >.

14. *Global Market Forecast for Internet Usage and Commerce,* International Data Corporation, July 1999.

15. *The Emerging Digital Economy,* U.S. Department of Commerce, 1998, p. 7.

16. Internet Usage and Commerce in Western Europe, 1997–2002. IDC report, 1998.

17. Gordon Moore has been unwilling to extend his "law" beyond 2010, because that is when current technologies will hit limits dictated by the size of the electron (see Moore, "Nanometers and Gigabucks—Moore on Moore's Law," *UVC Distinguished Lecture* 1996). At that point, the Semetech National Semiconductor Roadmap (1994) predicts that 450 times as many transistors will reside on a chip than in 1997. However, many observers anticipate that other technologies, such as optical computing, will extend the "law" much further into the future.

18. Gordon Bell and James N. Gray, "The Revolution Yet to Happen" in *Beyond Calculation: The Next Fifty Years in Computing*, edited by Peter J. Denning and Robert M. Metcalfe (New York: Copernicus Books, 1997), pp. 5–32.

19. As two well-qualified observers assert, "Fifty years from now computers will be as common and cheap as paper clips are today, and as little noticed." Peter J. Denning and Robert M. Metcalfe, "The Coming Revolution," in Denning and Metcalfe, ibid.

20. George Gilder: "Fiber Keeps its Promise" *Forbes ASAP* February 1997. The forecast that total bandwidth will triple every year for the next 25 years is often referred to as "Gilder's Law."

21. When we speak of a "thing" in this context, we mean physical things, including people. "Information" includes designs and creative work, not just data. The distinction between the economics of things and the economics of information has been made by a number of writers, most notably by Nicholas Negroponte in his essays for *Wired* magazine. (See *Being Digital* [New York: Alfred A. Knopf, 1995].) The most brilliantly original thinking on this is in the writings of Paul M. Romer. See his articles "Endogenous Technical Change," *Journal of Political Economy* 98, no. 5 (1990): S71–S102, and "Idea Gaps and Object Gaps in Economic Development," *Journal of Monetary Economics* 32 (1993): 543–573.

22. The architectural analogy is eloquently developed by George Gilder in *Life After Television* (New York: Norton, 1992).

23. Which is not obsolescence, of course. Book sales are much higher today than they were a century ago, and the lines to visit cathedrals may well be longer today than they were in the twelfth century.

24. Bookstores in general do not actually bear the cost of inventory: this is borne by the publisher. This has no effect on the economics of the business system, however.

25. The comparative stock market valuations of Peapod and Amazon.com may reflect this difference.

chapter three

1. This argument was first articulated in "Strategy and the New Economics of Information," by Philip B. Evans and Thomas S. Wurster. *Harvard Business Review* September–October 1997.

2. The concepts of "noise" and "garbling" in information theory are the engineering correlate of the trade-off between richness and reach. See Claude E. Shannon, "A Mathematical Theory of Communication," *Bell System Technical Journal,* 1948. It is interesting (and not coincidental) that the five-level, hierarchical switching structure of the Bell System as built in the fifties and sixties reflects Shannon's logic, in much the same ways that hierarchies in organization, choice, and relationship reflect the logic of richness and reach. For an excellent nontechnical survey of information theory, see John R. Pierce, *An Introduction to Information Theory: Symbols, Signals and Noise.* (New York: Dover Press, 1980).

3. This hierarchical structure to supply chains is most clearly evidenced in the automotive industry where the terms "tier one," "tier two," and so forth, are regularly applied to the manufacturers of components and subcomponents. The impact of the new economics of information on this hierarchical structure is discussed in chapter 9.

4. The logic of connectivity and standards, richness and reach, and the melting of the information glue is not specifically dependent on computers or the Internet. "Computers" are evolving into intelligent devices embedded in everything (prospectively, some say, even the human body). "The notion that all doors in a building should contain a computer chip seemed ludicrous 10 years ago, but now there is hardly a hotel door without a blinking beeping chip" (Kevin Kelly, *New Rules for the New Economy: 10 Radical Strategies for a Connected World,* Viking Press, 1998). This intelligence will be networked, based on connectivity and standards that may have nothing to do with TCP/IP. The networks will themselves be networked, perhaps using different connections and different standards. At some high level there will be a network of all networks that we will probably continue to call the "Internet." But the logic of richness and reach is by no means restricted to that high-level domain.

5. On railroad gauges specifically and standards in general see the excellent discussion by Carl Shapiro and Hal Varian, *Information Rules: A Strategic Guide to the Network Economy* (Boston: Harvard Business School Press, 1999), 208–210.

6. For a fascinating history of early computing see William Aspray, *John von Neumann and the Origins of Modern Computing* (Cambridge: The MIT Press, 1990).

7. On increasing returns and network externalities see W. Brian Arthur, *Increasing Returns and Path Dependence in the Economy* (Ann Arbor: University of Michigan Press, 1994). Increasing returns pose a challenge to "standard" economic theory, though this has long been recognized. See, for example, Alfred Marshall, *Principles of Economics* (8th edition), p. 459, and the classic article by Piero Sraffa, "The Laws of Returns under Competitive Conditions," *Economic Journal* vol. 26 (1926).

chapter four

1. See for example Roger Fidler, *Mediamorphosis: Understanding New Media* (Thousand Oaks, Calif.: Pine Forge Press, 1997).

2. The prototype customized electronic newspaper was developed at the MIT Media Lab and called "Fishwrap" after the journalist's proverb "Yesterday's news wraps today's fish." For a detailed description see < http://fishwrap-docs.www.media. mit.edu/docs/dev/CNGlue/cnglue.html >.

3. The most immediately vulnerable segment is job classifieds (especially for higher-skill jobs), which accounts for about one-third of classified revenues. The vulnerability of newspapers in the real estate and automotive categories is compounded by the vulnerabilities of realtors to disintermediation and of automotive dealers to a deconstruction of their own.

4. Bankers also argue, quite correctly, that some banking functions are irreducibly physical, such as dispensing cash or taking end-of-day cash deposits from business customers. Given current technologies, it is hard to see how these functions can be performed without some kind of distribution infrastructure. However, it is difficult to see how the distribution infrastructure of banks (ATMs apart) can be justified by the economics of these small (and frequently loss-making) activities. In a deconstructed world where these are seen as separate businesses, other players might prove more advantaged: supermarkets, for example.

5. If banking is destined for deconstruction, why the current frenzy of mega-mergers? There are three answers: One, traditional distribution-centered economics still count for a lot, and mergers are a means of shrinking capacity and wringing out the last increments of physical scale economies. Two, even in a deconstructed industry, large corporations may survive, provided they are run as loose federations of largely autonomous business units

(this is the structure of much of wholesale banking today); size may not do much good, but neither need it do any harm. Three, as the swamp dries up, the biggest dinosaurs stay alive longest; size is a smart strategy, if it is a *given* that you are a dinosaur.

6. CarMax Web site: <www.carmax.com>.

7. Amazon.com Web site: <www.amazon.com>.

chapter five

1. Disintermediation thus has two different meanings. One refers to those instances when the ultimate supplier of a good or service circumvents intermediaries and sells directly to the ultimate consumer. The second typically refers to the emergence of a new intermediary that employs a lower-cost way of distributing the good or service to try to displace existing intermediaries. Both meanings apply to the kinds of disintermediation we will explore in this chapter.

2. Patrick Spain and James Talbot, eds., *Hoover's Handbook of American Companies 1996* (Austin, Texas, Reference Press, 1995), p. 770.

3. This pattern of "new" disintermediation strongly echoes Clayton Christensen's brilliant account of the difficulties that incumbent competitors experience in dealing with "disruptive technologies." See Clayton M. Christensen, *The Innovator's Dilemma: When New Technologies Cause Great Firms to Fail* (Boston: Harvard Business School Press, 1997).

4. Ibid., p. 344.

5. Ibid., p. 344.

6. Ibid., p. 344.

7. Charles Schwab Corporation 10(k), 1995 and 1996, in SEC Filing Form 10-K Annual Report.

8. Matthew Schifrin, "Cyber-Schwab," *Forbes,* 5 May 1997, 42.

9. Excludes mutual fund trades, which distort numbers, according to Piper Jaffray. Piper Jaffray, "On-line Financial Services Update," March 1999.

10. *Statistical Abstract of the United States,* 1997, p. 768.

11. Karen Petska-Juliussen and Dr. Egil Juliussen, *The 8th Annual Computer Industry Almanac* (Austin, Texas, Reference Press, 1996), p. 505.

12. J&R Computer World and PC Mall advertisements, *PC Magazine,* August–December 1997.

13. Joan Margretta, "The Power of Vertical Integration: An Interview with Dell Computer's Michael Dell," *Harvard Business Review,* March–April 1998, 77.

14. These figures for days of inventory are constantly changing. All figures are from October 1998. Sources: *Computer Reseller News,* 5 October 1998 and 19 October 1998; *Money Magazine,* October 1998.

15. Deutsche Morgan Grenfell Technology Group, *The PC Industry* (Deutsche Morgan Grenfell, 1997).

16. Dell 10(k), April 1998, and 10(Q)s for first, second, and third quarters, 1999. SEC Filing Form10-K Annual Report, SEC Filing Form 10-Q Quarterly Report.

17. Joan Magretta, "The Power of Virtual Integration: An Interview with Dell Computer's Michael Dell," *Harvard Business Review,* March–April 1998. Michael Dell, *Direct from Dell* (HarperCollins, 1999), pp. 101–102, 157.

18. Peapod Web site: < www.peapod.com >.

19. Trade Dimensions, *Retail Tenant Directory* (Stamford: Interactive Market System, 1997).

20. *Forbes ASAP,* 23 February 1998, "Food Fighter," 37.

21. Evan Schwartz, "An Online Grocer Bets Against Bananas and Meat," *New York Times,* 4 May 1998.

22. Department of Commerce Report, *The Emerging Digital Economy,* 1998.

chapter six

1. Throughout this book we will use the word "supplier" to refer to the company that manufactures a good or provides a service. Many suppliers sell directly to the consumer; many sell through retailers.

2. The idea of bounded rationality and "satisficing" was introduced into economic thinking by Herbert Simon. See Herbert A. Simon, *Models of Man* (New York: Garland Publishing, 1957).

3. There are seven basic navigational functions: serving as a reposi-
tory of information, making a body of information comparable
and searchable, validating the accuracy of information, supply-
ing evaluation and advice, authenticating the identities of parties
involved in a transaction, providing a payment system, and guar-
anteeing the performance of one or both principals. Most intermediaries perform at least one of these functions, and thus are
considered navigators. It is not part of the definition of a navigator that it be a reseller of the product, but many are.

4. It is important not to overstate this argument. While there are
some examples of leading brands gaining share in the context of
increasing clutter, there are also examples of where this did not
happen. The leading television networks have continued to lose
share as cable channels have proliferated. Amazon.com sells proportionately fewer bestsellers and more "midlist" than does the
book industry as a whole. In every case, pro and con, there are
special factors that could explain the phenomenon. The hypothesis that top brands gain from clutter is just that: a hypothesis.

5. Shop.org study in conjunction with The Boston Consulting
Group, November 1998.

6. Barnes & Noble and Borders 10(Q)s, October 1998; Books-a-
Million 1998 10(k), SEC Filing Form 10-K Annual Report, SEC
Filing For 10-Q Quarterly Report; "Are Independents Making a
Comeback? (booksellers)," *Publisher's Weekly*, 8 June 1998, 21.

7. The Dell Web site offers consumer desktop choices for the system, memory, hard drive, video card, TV tuner, DVD/CD-ROM
drive, sound card, speakers, modem, and zip drives. There are
also choices for accessories such as virus protection software,
keyboard, and mouse. This comparison is a bit unfair, since any
computer store would be willing to customize memory and
peripherals in accordance with customers' wishes.

8. But of course everything else is not equal. Agency affiliation and
richness are also key dimensions of advantage that will be discussed in chapters 7 and 8, respectively.

9. The term "Metcalfe's Law" was coined by George Gilder in 1993
(< http://www.discovery.org/gilder/metcalf.html >) though Bob
Metcalfe has protested that he was merely trying to sell Ethernet
technology.

10. The power of Metcalfe's "law" is illustrated by the scientific publishing industry, which may be the ultimate network business. A year's subscription to *Atherosclerosis* costs $2,700. Scientific journals earn margins comparable to those of classified advertising. Researchers provide the raw material *for free*, because they must publish in the highest-status journals, or perish. Faculty chairmen are *honored* to serve for free on editorial review panels. Researchers *must* keep up with the latest research. University librarians *must* provide the journals the faculty request, and have therefore made draconian cuts in purchases of monographs to maintain continuity in their journal subscriptions. The major value-added by the publisher is actually negative: typesetting and printing hold up publication by six to twelve months, this in an industry where timely dissemination is often critical. Competition among publishers is negligible because each journal is an established intellectual "marketplace" for its field: as publication volume grows, new journals emerge not as competitors, but focused on subspecialties. Writers contribute because the readers are there and subscribers read because the writers are there. Resentment against the publishers is strong, but everybody plays the game *because everybody else does.*

Electronic publishing raises the obvious specter of disintermediation. The suppliers, peer reviewers, and readers all have access to the Net; indeed they are precisely the same people. Since they do all the work for free anyway, they could disintermediate the publishers and collectively save about $2 billion a year, this in an industry that is desperately short of funds. Publication could be instantaneous. But so strong is the network effect that no serious inroads have been made into the monopoly of the scientific publishing industry. As costs head towards zero, margins head towards infinity.

11. CareerPath.com was cofounded in 1995 by the *Boston Globe, Chicago Tribune, Los Angeles Times, New York Times, San Jose Mercury News,* and *Washington Post.*

chapter seven

1. Seller-paid navigators do not always pursue sellers' interests. Moody's and Standard & Poor's rate bond risks from the investor's point of view despite that fact that the borrower pays them. None of this argument implies that any seller-affiliated navigator *ignores* the buyers' needs or interests: that is precisely how the

sale is made. The point is simply that, for instance, a good sales-person or a successful advertising campaign is measured not by the extent to which it helps customers to fulfill needs, but by the revenues that it generates.

2. Specificity is the main reason for vertical integration: when two activities can succeed only through a high degree of mutual dependence, co-ownership is likely. Agency affiliation is a weak form of vertical integration. The concept of specificity was developed by Oliver Williamson. See his *Markets and Hierarchies: Analysis and Antitrust Implications* (New York: Free Press, 1975).

3. This is what game theorists call a prisoner's dilemma.

4. American Airlines was eventually forced by industry and governmental pressure to stop the practice of presenting schedule information to favor its own flights. This eliminated a competitive advantage for the airline but also eliminated a competitive *disadvantage* for SABRE. Since SABRE the navigator is now a business twice as valuable as AA the airline, the shareholders probably benefited.

5. There is another problem. With time, dominant navigators will learn how to auction off finely graded distinctions in seller positioning and presentation. The best positioning will be sold off to the seller to whom it is worth most; slightly inferior positioning will be sold to the second-highest bidder, and so forth. Much of the value of navigational positioning could thus be extracted *by the navigator*, just as the owners of sports broadcasting rights extract from advertisers the full value of the mass audience that they are uniquely able to deliver.

chapter eight

1. This is not merely a central issue for the relationships among suppliers, retailers, and customers. The ability to add richness is also critical to the future of supply chains and organizations—topics that we will discuss in later chapters.

2. Boston Consulting Group, "Seeds of Deconstruction," 12 December 1998.

3. Technology for tracking customer behavior to define customer segments and extrapolate individual preferences was first commercialized by a company called Firefly, which was acquired by Microsoft in 1998.

4. Robert D. Hof, Heather Green, and Linda Himelstein, "Now It's Your Web," *BusinessWeek,* 5 October 1998.

5. Software navigators or agents will soon employ sophisticated techniques to *learn* through usage about their principal's behavior and preferences, drawing from the techniques of artificial intelligence. The more such software knows, the better it will serve its principal's interests. But for that very reason, people will have an ever-more-powerful incentive to *own* such agents, rather than allow some third party to provide agency services and thereby acquire (and possibly misuse) such rich and sensitive knowledge. As the cost (and therefore scale threshold) of the underlying technology falls, so the consumer's scale disadvantage against the intermediary will diminish, while the affiliation logic for owning the agent will become ever more compelling. If some parts of the navigational function are pulled by different forces from others, those differences will simply drive further deconstruction.

6. The value of a customer-generated information file is lowered by the possibility of deliberate self-misrepresentation. However, if this were the only problem, there would be easy technological fixes.

7. This idea is fully developed in John Hagel III and Marc Singer, *Net Worth: Shaping Markets When Customers Make the Rules* (Boston: Harvard Business School Press, 1999).

8. Our colleagues Stuart Scantlebury and David Ritter pointed out that the value chain of music making itself has been the object of a technological deconstruction that exactly parallels the patterns we see in business. It is driven, as always, by the advent of connectivity and standards.

   Music making is information making. The performer, the instrument, and the resulting sound are as vertically integrated as any value chain in the business world. The electronic synthesizer, invented by Robert Moog in the 1960s, used analogue technology to synthesize sounds by combining waveforms. The output was an electrical signal that could be fed directly into a mixer or amplifier, disintermediating the microphone. But it was *just another instrument*, with its own vertically integrated value chain. Since different units had different, proprietary capabilities, performers would have to transport, set up, and play half a dozen synthesizers in a performance. New sounds, but old economics.

In the early 1980s, MIDI (the Musical Instrument Digital Interface) was developed as a standard to define musical information. A keyboard (serving as a "MIDI controller") would generate instructions in terms of pitch, duration, and attack. An output device (a "MIDI instrument") would combine these instructions with sampled sounds to produce an analog signal for the mixer or amplifier. Not as much creative control as the real thing, but *good enough*. By connecting a controller to multiple MIDI instruments, a single performer could sound like a band.

MIDI controllers proliferated: guitars, drums, even "MIDI wind." So did specialist output devices: drum machines, effects processors, even modules for lighting and fireworks. One standard built on another: successive standards specified an instrument schema, more special effects, absolute synchronization (for movie making), and formats for downloading sounds over the Internet.

Software was developed to enable PCs to translate back and forth between MIDI and conventional musical notation. This enabled amateurs and professionals variously and simultaneously to compose, record, edit, and perform any of the separate instrumental tracks in an ensemble piece.

The impact on musicians' productivity was stunning. Music copyists and score writers have become nearly extinct. Musicians can compose and perform complex music well beyond their skill level on real-time instruments. Large bands were replaced by three piece combos. Singers and pianists dispensed with their bassists and drummers. In the early 1990s in Las Vegas and New York, musicians went on strike against MIDI— unsuccessfully.

9. This is a literal quote from the product brochure for a high-end stereo loudspeaker system.

10. Philosophers might distinguish "brand as denotation" from "brand as connotation."

11. Even Sony and Coca-Cola are not pure cases. Part of the Sony brand is its aura of upscale sophistication. Part of the Coca-Cola brand is the belief that it always tastes the same.

12. Ignoring patent and copyright issues.

chapter nine

1. Extranets are not technically distinct from the Internet. They may be defined as closed networks (i.e., requiring a password)

that use Internet communication protocols. They may or may not run over the physical Internet structure, but whether they do or not is not important to this discussion.

2. ANX Web site: <www.anxo.com>.

3. Interview with Doug Buchanan, Business Technology Manager, Dofasco Inc.

4. Interview with Bryan Whittle at Bellcore, official overseer of ANX.

5. Interview with Fred Hakim at Chrysler.

6. Based on documentation found in the "Manufacturing Assembly Pilot (MAP) Project Final Report" provided by the Automotive Industry Action Group.

7. CIMSOURCE Web site: <www.cimsource.com>.

8. On this theme, see Carliss Y. Baldwin and Kim Clark, "Managing in an Age of Modularity," *Harvard Business Review* September–October 1997.

9. RosettaNet Web site: <www.rosettanet.org>.

10. Ibid.

11. Boston Consulting Group, "Managing for a Wired Health Care Industry," *INVIVO*, July/August 1996.

12. According to one estimate, $276 billion is wasted annually on unneeded and duplicated treatments or through administrative inefficiency. Not all of this can be attributed to constraints on information flows. See the report "Health Care On Line" by Jay Rosenbuth et al., Bedrock Capital Partners (out of print).

13. For hepatitis C, the Hepatitis Connections Web site (<http://hepatitis-c.de/linkse.htm>) lists 33 general sources, 14 personal help sites, 12 research institutes, 6 journals, 8 societies, 18 organizations, 12 newsgroups, 54 overseas resources, and 19 sites supporting further search.

14. Decision Innovations literature.

15. Smart cards carrying patient records are already in various stages of implementation in Spain, France, and the Czech Republic.

16. See Regina Herzlinger, *Market Driven Health Care: Who Wins, Who Loses in the Transformation of America's Largest Service Indus-*

try (Boston: Harvard Business School Press, 1997). For an excellent discussion of the impact of technology on health care see Michael L. Millenson, *Demanding Medical Excellence: Doctors and Accountability in the Information Age* (Chicago: The University of Chicago Press, 1997).

chapter ten

1. Throughout the 1980s the Japanese corporation (indeed the Japanese corporate system) was widely viewed as a superior model of management. Many scholars focused on organization as the key to Japan's competitive success and raised serious questions about the health of the Western-style corporation. (See, for example, Ezra F. Vogel, *Japan as Number One* [Cambridge: Harvard University Press, 1979], or William G. Ouchi, *Theory Z: How American Business Can Meet the Japanese Challenge* [Reading, MA: Addison-Wesley, 1981]). This view was overstated: it mistook the excellence of a small number of engineering-intensive, export-focused companies for that of an entire economic system, and it failed to recognize that even in those companies, their peculiar methods of management suited them for some kinds of tasks, and strategy, but not for others. However, what has happened in the past ten years is not that the excellences identified by those organizational scholars have proved false or ephemeral, but rather that the macroeconomy has shifted. It is no longer those sectors, and no longer those strategies within those sectors, that suffice for global competitiveness. But the excellences are still there. Both the exaggeration of the eighties and the deflation of the nineties are unwarranted.

2. Cultural variations in richness and reach, their implications for social structures, and the possibilities of deconstruction under the new economics of information would merit the attention of a separate book.

3. At the height of Japan's real estate boom, these districts were reputed to enjoy a total real estate valuation greater than that of California. Whether high land prices are a *cause* or a *consequence* of the apparent Japanese managerial preference for intimate colocation is an interesting matter for debate, unrelated to our central argument. Certainly to the extent that Japanese managerial methods are grounded in national "character" (most famously captured by Ruth Benedict in *The Chrysanthemum and the Sword*)

and national character has its origins in the imperatives of cooperative rice farming in self-contained villages, everything is explained by "the land."

4. For an excellent description of this and other aspects of the traditional postwar Japanese corporation, written from the viewpoint of a trained anthropologist, see Thomas P. Rohlen, *For Harmony and Strength: Japanese White-Collar Organization in Anthropological Perspective* (Berkeley, CA: University of California Press, 1974).

5. This was the view classically argued by Adolf A. Berle and Gardiner C. Means in *Modern Corporation and Private Property* (New York: Harcourt, Brace & World, 1968).

6. The much-remarked novelty and success of Thermo Electron (at least until very recently) contrasts with its curious lack of imitators. For a description of the company's managerial style (which is somewhere between those of a venture capital firm and a conglomerate), see "Spinning It Out at Thermo Electron," *The Economist,* 12 April 1997.

7. Pamela Mendels P. Entiz, "Now That's Casting a Wide Net," *BusinessWeek,* 25 May 1998.

8. On the deconstruction of labor markets, see Thomas W. Malone and Robert J Laubacher, "The Dawn of the E-Lance Economy," *Harvard Business Review* September–October 1998.

9. James Kirk, "2 Game Plans in MJ's Nike Deal with Jordan Line," *Chicago Tribune,* 10 September 1997.

10. Management accounting and control systems implicitly assume that the key source of value creation is capital, not labor. As our colleague Felix Barber has demonstrated in work as yet unpublished, the premise that *labor* is the key and constraining factor of production leads to fundamentally different metrics for performance measurement and resource allocation.

11. Analee Saxenian, *Regional Advantage: Culture and Competition in Silicon Valley and Route 128* (Cambridge: Harvard University Press, 1994), p.35.

12. Ibid., p. 36.

13. The application of biological analogies to late capitalism is emphasized by a number of writers, incuding Michael Rothschild, *Bionomics: The Inevitability of Capitalism* (New York: Henry

Holt and Company, 1995), and Kevin Kelly, *Out of Control: The Rise of Neo-Biological Civilization* (Reading, Mass.: Addison-Wesley, 1994).

14. See Frances Cairncross, *The Death of Distance* (Boston: Harvard Business School Press, 1997).

15. See, for example, Jessica Lipnack and Jeffrey Stamps, *Virtual Teams: Reaching Across Space, Time and Organizations with Technology* (New York: John Wiley, 1997).

16. On this point see the excellent discussion by Jonathan D. Day and James C. Wendler, "The New Economics of Organization," *McKinsey Quarterly*, no. 1 (1998).

17. On shareholder value management, see James A. Knight, *Value Based Management: Developing a Systematic Approach to Creating Shareholder Value* (New York: McGraw-Hill, 1997) and Boston Consulting Group, "Shareholder Value Management—Shareholder Value Metrics," 1996.

18. The implicit analogy between organization and software cuts much deeper and extends to many information technologies. We have described in the context of business the logic of deconstruction and the substitution of self-organizing, modular systems for centrally controlled hierarchies. We have applied this to value chains, supply chains, consumer search (and therefore to franchises and brands), the relation between the corporation and its stakeholders, and patterns of collaboration within and among corporations. Exactly the same logic applies to technologies. Packet-switched telecommunications networks are a "deconstructed" substitute for the hierarchical, circuit-switched networks developed by AT&T in the 1950s. Object-oriented programming techniques are a deconstructed substitute for the hierarchical top-down programming methods employed in the 1970s. Browsers and databases, clients and servers, variously collaborating over the Internet using Java, Jini, or ActiveX, are a deconstructed substitute for the traditional computing environment in which all tasks are performed on one machine within the layered software hierarchy defined by a conventional operating system. Centerless, intelligent networks of smart devices in the home (as envisaged in Sony's HAVI architecture and Aperios operating system) are a deconstructed substitute for the PC-centric home network defended by Microsoft and Intel. So-called component software—small software objects often downloaded as needed

(such as Java applets)—are a deconstructed substitute for $300 shrink-wrapped packages.

In every case, the older, hierarchical architecture is more "efficient" by some static measure. In every case, technology has rendered static efficiency less important. It has also rendered adaptability, scalability, and fault tolerance *more* important. The key advantages of self-organizing, modular systems (both technological and human) are precisely that they are adaptable, scalable, and fault-tolerant.

19. The parallel logic of "deconstruction" in social and political arenas is developed by Francis Fukuyama in *Trust: The Social Virtues and the Creation of Prosperity* (New York: Free Press, 1995). See also Albert O. Hirschman's classic essay *Exit, Voice and Loyalty: Responses to Decline in Firms, Organizations and States* (Boston: Harvard University Press, 1970).

Index

aвoυt тнe aυтнoRs

Philip Evans is a Senior Vice President in The Boston Consulting Group's Boston office and coleader of BCG's Media and Convergence practice group. His consulting practice is focused on strategy issues for clients in the media, financial services, and consumer goods industries. He is the coauthor of three articles published in the *Harvard Business Review,* including "Strategy and the New Economics of Information," and a frequent speaker on the new economics of information. Prior to joining BCG he obtained the top double first class honours degree from Cambridge University in economics. He was subsequently a Harkness Fellow in the economics department at Harvard University and obtained an M.B.A. from the Harvard Business School. He can be reached at evans.philip@bcg.com.

Thomas S. Wurster is a Vice President with The Boston Consulting Group and leads the Los Angeles office. He is also coleader of BCG's Media and Convergence practice group. His consulting practice is focused on working with leading media, consumer products, and e-commerce companies. He writes on media and strategy and is the coauthor of two articles published in the *Harvard Business Review,* including the prize-winning "Strategy and the New Economics of Information." He is a graduate of Cornell University, where he earned an A.B. in economics and mathematics with distinction. He received his M.B.A. with honors from the University of Chicago and earned his Ph.D. in economics from Yale University. He can be reached at wurster.tom@bcg.com.